Protecting Intellectual Property

Protecting Intellectual Property

Understanding and using trade marks, patents, design and copyright in business

---

Richard Halstead

B.Sc., M.I.T.M.A., C.P.A.
Chartered Patent Attorney &
Registered Trade Mark Agent

ICSA Publishing
The Official Publishing Company of
The Institute of Chartered Secretaries and Administrators

First published 1993 by
ICSA Publishing Limited
Campus 400, Maylands Avenue
Hemel Hempstead
Hertfordshire, HP2 7EZ

Typeset in 10/12pt Palatino
by Keyset Composition, Colchester, Essex

Printed and bound in Great Britain by
Hartnolls, Bodmin, Cornwall

British Library Cataloguing in Publication Data

A catalogue record for this book is available from the British Library

ISBN 0-902197-64-9 (hbk)

1 2 3 4 5 97 96 95 94 93

Contents

Introduction

This book deals with the subject of intellectual property from the perspective of the business manager and has the object of imparting sufficient knowledge to the reader for providing a framework within which commercial decisions relating to intellectual property can be made. The ever-growing demand for increasingly sophisticated products and services combined with the general worldwide trend of lowering barriers to free trade means that a knowledge and understanding of intellectual property is an essential prerequisite to successful modern business.

Intellectual property is undeniably complex. This means that those persons directly affected by it, people in business, must usually rely upon advice given by professional legal advisers such as solicitors, chartered patent agents and registered trade mark agents. However, although such advisers must devote many years of hard work and study to understand fully the intricacies of intellectual property law, this is often to the exclusion of even a basic understanding of how companies remain profitable in an ever-competitive world.

It is hoped that this book will at least partially bridge the gap between, on the one hand, a complete lack of understanding of intellectual property and thus total reliance upon the advice of others and, on the other, having to become thoroughly acquainted with the subject at the expense of the precious time needed to run a profitable business.

The book has been divided roughly into two parts. The first six chapters explain the different kinds of intellectual property rights available including patents, registered trade marks, registered designs and copyrights, and how they are obtained. Readers with a rudimentary knowledge of the various forms of intellectual property may wish to skip these chapters, although it is recommended that Chapter 1 be read, since it sets out certain ground rules which are essential to the proper understanding and management of intellectual property. Chapters 7 to 14 then look at a range of topics which are consequential on the establishment of intellectual property rights including enforcement, exploitation by means of licensing, sale or franchise, costs, clearance searches, valuation and taxation. The final chapter deals specifically with the European Common Market and the significant effect it has upon the subject of intellectual property as it relates to business practices.

Finally, a word about the style and presentation of this book. Intellectual property law as a subject is too wide-ranging to be compressed into a single volume and, in any event, it is not the intention of the author to provide anything other than a brief guide to a large number of topics so that a basic understanding of each can be obtained relatively easily and quickly. For this reason the book contains very few references to specific legal statutes or case law, it being considered preferable to condense established legal principles into the more readily understandable but nevertheless equally accurate language used by people in everyday life. There are, however, five appendices which the reader may find it useful to refer to including a published patent specification, an extract from the UK *Trade Marks Journal* showing how accepted trade mark applications are advertised for possible opposition by third parties, a trade mark registration certificate and a design registration certificate. Collectively, this material constitutes tangible evidence of the intangible nature of intellectual property rights.

Acknowledgement

I owe grateful thanks to the help and forbearance given by my wife, Ruth, during the production of this book.

1 Basic concepts

Intellectual property is sometimes also referred to as 'industrial property' but because this can also include tangible forms of property, such as real estate, it is perhaps a less appropriate term and will not be used in this book.

The concept of intellectual property can be viewed as being derived from a recognition that it is desirable to prevent unfairness in business. Such unfairness may be the result of one person copying the original literary work of another and claiming it for himself, or at least exploiting it by publishing and making a profit from such publication. A research worker may spend many years developing a new product or process to a point at which it becomes commercially valuable, only to find that upon news of the invention being made public competitors take the fruits of his labours for free. A manufacturer may produce goods of excellent quality and identify them by reference to a trade mark upon which the purchasing public come to rely as meaning a badge of quality, only to find a competitor adopting the same or a confusingly similar trade mark on goods of inferior quality, so that a hard-won reputation disappears almost overnight.

These are just a couple of examples which illustrate why it is necessary to provide laws which prevent such acts of unfair competition or exploitation in their many forms.

Although the basic idea behind intellectual property law is relatively simple, putting it into effect is not. The law must provide a balance between granting too much protection to the extent that fair competition is stifled, and providing insufficient protection so as to discourage investment in new technologies or high quality branded products and the like. Because of the diverse nature of intellectual property, ranging from technology-related rights to purely artistic rights, from marketing tools such as trade marks and trade names to plant breeders' rights, there is no common theme running through all, other than the basic recognition that unfair competition or unfair exploitation should not be tolerated.

Before discussing briefly the various kinds of intellectual property available it is useful to examine the basic structure of the legal framework within which we must all operate and within which intellectual property law as it exists in the United Kingdom is framed.

The legal framework

Statute law

Within the United Kingdom there are essentially two legal systems, each operating in tandem, but being derived very differently. The first is the statute law, which is the set of laws written down and approved by Parliament. Each law or 'Act of Parliament' usually deals with a specific range of subject matter; for instance, the Theft Act states amongst other things that it is unlawful for one person to steal another person's property. This Act also includes many other provisions including maximum penalties for various kinds of theft. It contains the complete written law relating to theft (although there are some exceptions) and thus provides a rigid structure of what is considered acceptable behaviour to be imposed upon society in general by virtue of that particular Act of Parliament. Similarly, Parliament has enacted laws which relate to intellectual property and which provide a fully codified framework within which the law relating to, for example, patents, registered designs and copyrights is contained.

Common law

The other side of the coin is the common law which is a set of laws that are not expressly approved by Parliament but are nevertheless followed by the Courts. The common law, as a body of law, has been built up over many centuries and generally relies upon a Court recognizing what has been decided in previous similar cases, unless the subject matter in question has since been brought under one of the Acts of Parliament (i.e. one of the statute laws). For example, the Courts have for many years held that it is wrong for one person to trespass upon the property of another without permission. Although there is still no statutory law preventing this, nevertheless the Court will, if asked, issue an injunction to stop a trespasser from repeating the offence. In doing so, the Court will be relying upon precedents found in previous cases of a similar nature (the 'case law') relative to that particular subject. Similarly, certain aspects of intellectual property are protected solely by the common law, such as the law relating to 'passing off' one trader's goods as those of another trader, as will be explained later.

What all of this means is that, depending upon the nature of the intellectual property, it is sometimes necessary to consider either solely statute law or solely common law, and sometimes both.

External influences on the law

Then we have the external influences on the internal law of the United Kingdom. These are generally international treaties or conventions to which the United Kingdom has become a signatory and which have as their effect the development and evolution of UK law. Examples are the Treaty of Rome, by which the European Economic Community was established, and the General Agreement on Tariffs and Trade (the GATT). These external influences often transcend the boundaries of national legislation so that when one collides with the other, more often than not it is the national legislation which has to give way.

The Treaty of Rome

The effect of the Treaty of Rome on intellectual property law is discussed in detail in Chapter 15 but it may be useful to summarize briefly here how it impinges upon intellectual property law in the United Kingdom.

Since the EEC has always adopted the principle of open competition and free trade (at least theoretically so) between member states, it will be immediately apparent that the exercise of an intellectual property right can effectively undermine this principle. The owner of a patent (the 'patentee') for a product or a process can exclude competitors from making use of the patented technology so that he has an effective monopoly.

The same may be true of a trade mark owner who would naturally wish to sell products bearing the trade mark throughout the whole of the EEC. By registering the mark in all member states, the owner usually establishes a monopoly over the use of the mark and any other mark which is confusingly similar in relation to the goods or services for which the mark has been registered. There is no particular problem with this provided no one else within the Community already uses the same or a similar mark. However, problems arise where an identical or similar mark is already being legitimately used by someone else in another member state.

A compromise therefore has to be reached between the principle of open competition and free trade and the principle of preventing unfair competition and unfair trading practices by granting intellectual property rights. The compromise for the Treaty of Rome is generally that open competition and free trade within member states of the Community is usually subject to the existence of intellectual property rights in each member state. The compromise for intellectual property owners is that monopolistic and similar rights sometimes cannot be exercised if the effect would amount to a distortion of trade extending beyond the primary or immediate subject matter of the intellectual property right concerned.

Re-importation

To illustrate what is meant by this take the situation whereby the manufacturer of a product sells it in the United Kingdom at one price, but because of local market considerations sells the same product in another member state at a lower price. In such circumstances, the trade mark owner cannot prevent the re-importation (commonly called 'parallel importation') of those same products which have been legitimately purchased by a third party in another member state. He is therefore unable to prevent the third party from selling the products on the open market in the United Kingdom at a lower price than the 'genuine' UK product. The usual right to control the use of the trade mark on the product cannot be exercised and is thus said to be exhausted once the product is legitimately put onto the EEC market by the trade mark owner. This 'exhaustion of rights' principle thus establishes a cut-off point for intellectual property owners preventing them from departing too far from the open competition and free trade principles of the EEC.

Abuse of a dominant position

Similarly, another cut-off point arises when there is an abuse of a dominant position held by one or several business enterprises operating within the Community. This does not always mean an abuse of a dominant position relating to an intellectual property right and can include situations whereby cartels are formed to maintain prices artificially. The owner of an intellectual property right can abuse a dominant position by exerting an influence over open competition and free trade extending beyond the specific subject matter of the granted intellectual property right. For example, the owner of patented technology may decide to license it to one or several competitors within the EEC. Requiring each licensee also to purchase raw materials not covered by the patent from a specified source such as the patentee is a clear abuse of a dominant position and whilst this, in itself, cannot be used as a ground for revoking the patent in each member state to which the patent rights extend, the Treaty of Rome nevertheless provides that in such circumstances the owner of the patent can no longer exercise control over the patented technology within the EEC. He loses his rights by abusing them.

Thus, UK and other national legislation relating to intellectual property rights within the EEC affects and is affected by Community law.

The GATT

The General Agreement on Tariffs and Trade is not quite as interactive with national intellectual property laws but nevertheless recognizes that in order for there to be fair trading practices between member countries of the GATT, there has to be adequate intellectual property protection in each country. The lack of such protection generally excludes membership from the GATT and has been successfully used to force countries such as China to alter and improve their internal intellectual property protection in order to qualify for membership status.

Even so, despite the suggestion given by its name, members of the GATT are not in general agreement as to what constitutes a satisfactory level of intellectual property protection. They can be divided roughly into two camps: in the first are the highly developed nations who insist upon a substantial level of protection being given to owners of trade marks, copyrights, design rights and patented technology including granting patent protection for pharmaceutical products. In the other camp are the less developed countries who generally adopt less sophisticated and hence less comprehensive systems of intellectual property protection. For example, trade mark rights are often granted on a first-to-file basis rather than by recognition of the prior rights of the original trade mark owner to register a mark in preference to, usually, local parties who adopt and register the same mark in full knowledge that by doing so an unfair commercial advantage is obtained. Similarly, fewer kinds of inventions are considered patentable and most notably there is a lack of patent protection for pharmaceutical products in many of these countries. The justification for this stems from the high prices drug companies charge for their products, making it difficult for impoverished nations to afford the most up-to-date drugs without allowing access to the technology by local manufacturers.

From the foregoing, it will be apparent that intellectual property protection is not uniform around the world and that in some countries almost no protection exists at all.

Categories of intellectual property

Intellectual property can be broadly categorized into five main areas, although some of them intermingle. There are also other kinds of intellectual property which cannot be so easily categorized, such as plant breeder's rights, which are unlikely to interest the average reader and hence are not discussed further in this book. Three of the five main categories can be regarded as monopolistic in their nature whereas the remaining two are not. These three are patents (for inventions), trade marks and registered designs. The two non-monopolistic categories are copyright (including the recently introduced Design Right) and confidential information or 'know-how'.

Monopolistic categories

It should be noted that with regard to the first three, the monopoly is really quite limited in that it does not give to the owner in each case the *right* to exploit an invention, trade mark or design, as the case may be, but merely the right to prevent others from doing so. Even then, this limited right can be eroded further, particularly in the case of patents, by the right of the government to use an invention with or without the agreement of the owner. Third parties may also obtain licences under a patent in the event that the patented technology is being under-utilized by the patentee, or in the event that the existence of the patent prevents or inhibits commercial exploitation of other technology.

Despite these limitations, ownership of a patent, trade mark or registered design can provide a very powerful weapon with which the owner can, if he so wishes, effectively exclude competition for a limited period, in respect of patents and registered designs, and for an unlimited period in respect of trade marks.

Non-monopolistic categories

Copyright means precisely what it says, i.e. it is the right to stop another person from copying the 'work' of the original author. Qualifying works comprise books, operas, music, plays, films, photographs, paintings, engineering drawings (now protected by the new Design Right discussed in Chapter 5) and even computer programs. Copyright is infringed by someone who copies the work to a substantial extent, meaning that the infringer is unlikely to escape penalties for infringement by making only minor changes to a copyright work. However, an act of copying is required in order to infringe copyright and thus the copyright law cannot be used to prevent the exploitation of original works which are derived honestly and independently.

Perhaps surprisingly, confidential know-how is often a very valuable form of intellectual property right, particularly in relation to process industries such as steel and glass manufacturing where even small increases in efficiency nevertheless translate into significant cost savings over time. For know-how to constitute a form of intellectual property it must be kept secret and whilst it remains so it can be licensed to third parties for a royalty fee, usually under terms of strict confidence. Know-how rights are a type of technical trade secret by which products and processes can be made or operated more efficiently in terms of cost saving or quality, and disappear as soon as the trade secret becomes publicly known. There is no system for registering know-how and the remedy for the owner of the know-how in the event that a licensee discloses it to an unauthorized third party is a lawsuit for breach of contract.

Conclusion

These five general categories collectively represent perhaps the most important set of laws which provide for fair competition in business. Knowing what the laws are and how they can be exploited has become increasingly important to those involved in managing businesses. With the increasingly technical sophistication of modern business this trend is likely to continue.

The Paris Convention

Finally, this chapter on basic concepts also requires a brief discussion on another treaty which has a significant and practical benefit for anyone interested in obtaining patents, registered trade marks and registered designs. This treaty is familiarly referred to as the Paris Convention and has been ratified by a large number of countries, although there are some notable exceptions such as Taiwan and Thailand. Signatory countries to the convention agree to grant and recognize the rights of foreigners to obtain patents, trade marks and designs on the basis of reciprocity, subject to any national laws to the contrary. For example, Article 6*bis* of the convention requires that each signatory state should recognize the existence of internationally famous trade marks and ensure that trade mark protection is only given to the genuine trade mark owner. Whilst there is, obviously, enormous room for argument as to what constitutes a 'famous trade mark', nevertheless this general principle can be exploited to good effect by trade mark owners who find that their mark has already been registered in a particular country by someone else – but only if the mark in question is truly famous in the international sense.

Benefits of membership

A major benefit to membership of the Paris Convention lies in the fact that it requires member states to recognize rights of priority of residents in other member states who have previously applied for patents, registered designs and registered trade marks, usually in their own country. This priority right can be exercised up to 6 months after the filing of an original application to register a trade mark or a design, and up to 12 months in respect of an application to obtain a patent. A significant advantage of this scheme lies in the fact that without it an applicant for a patent, for example, would have to file a patent application in each and every member country where such protection was required more or less at the same moment in time, or otherwise run the risk that news of the invention for which a patent is being sought becomes publicly disclosed, thereby preventing the grant of a valid patent in each country.

Patents

In the case of patents, this 12-month grace period therefore provides a very useful buffer which dispenses with the need to simultaneously file a large number of technically complex documents in each country where patents are required, and pay the legal fees involved, at a point in time when the invention may still have to prove its worth in commercial terms. This means that if, say, a UK manufacturer were to invent a new product then initially it would only be necessary to apply for the patent in the United Kingdom and there would then be a 12-month grace period for filing corresponding patent applications elsewhere (apart from Taiwan and Thailand). Logistically, this makes matters more manageable and, of course, keeps costs to a minimum during the early stages of exploiting the invention.

Trade marks and designs

The same considerations apply with regard to the registration of trade marks and designs, the 6-month grace period reflecting the fact that the filing of applications to register these two forms of intellectual property is generally less complex and expensive than for obtaining a patent. Even so, knowing that an application for registration of a trade mark filed at the UK Trade Marks Registry will thereby provide an option to do further market research in other territories, including carrying out searches to determine if other parties have already registered similar marks in those territories, whilst still allowing sufficient time to file applications for registration elsewhere within the 6-month period, provides a useful managerial tool for optimimizing manpower and financial resources.

The Paris Convention should therefore be seen as a friend of management which provides flexibility for those interested in acquiring intellectual property rights.

2 Patents and how to obtain them

Background

Historically, patents used to be granted only by the ruling monarch and did not always concern new technology. The Royal Letters Patent comprised in each case a declaration by the king or queen to the effect that the recipient of the patent was entitled to certain privileges and rights over and above the common citizenry. In England, the first true patent was granted to John of Utynam in 1449 by King Henry VI for a new method of making stained-glass windows for Eton College. The second patent was granted in 1552 and also concerned glass manufacture.

Considerable refinement of the patent system has occurred over the years which has resulted in the very sophisticated and complex patent system now in use in the United Kingdom. The same kind of changes have occurred in many other countries so that whilst there is still no such thing as a worldwide patent, nevertheless it would not take a great deal of effort in terms of legislative amendments to provide a unitary patent covering a reasonably comprehensive list of developed countries. In European terms this object may eventually be achieved by the implementation of the Community Patent Convention which is intended to provide a single patent covering a variety of member states. The trouble is that national laws have tended to get in the way of this objective and it seems unlikely that a unified patent system will exist in Europe for several years at least.

Whilst a worldwide patent may yet be many years away, however, moves have already been made to at least streamline and simplify the process of obtaining patents, perhaps the best example of this being the European Patent Convention which results in what is misleadingly termed a 'European patent'. At the time of writing there were 17 member states to this Convention, which permits the filing of a single patent application, at the European Patent Office in Munich or one of its branches at The Hague or the Patent Office in Newport, Wales. These are Austria, Belgium, Denmark, France, Germany, Greece, Ireland, Italy, Liechtenstein, Luxembourg, Monaco, the Netherlands, Portugal, Spain, Sweden, Switzerland and the United Kingdom.

The European patent application undergoes only one examination procedure prior to a decision being made as to whether or not to grant the patent. If the patent is granted then it results in it being 'adopted' as a national patent by each of the states designated on the application form, subject to the completion of certain national formalities such as the filing of translations at each national patent office.

What is a patent?

A patent can be viewed as being a bargain reached between the State and an inventor (or an employer of the inventor) whereby in return for full disclosure of the new invention the State will *possibly* grant a monopoly over the exploitation of the invention for up to 20 years from the filing date, provided the invention qualifies for a patent. To qualify, an invention must be new and must not be an obvious improvement over the existing technological art (the 'prior art') within which the invention falls.

Definition of newness

The test for newness (or novelty) is absolute in that unless priority can be claimed from an earlier filing in another member state under the Paris Convention, no public disclosure of the invention whatsoever must have been made anywhere in the world. This could include accidental or deliberate disclosure by the inventor but, more usually, includes disclosure by an unrelated third party who may have invented or suggested the same invention in a previously filed patent application or some other publicly available document such as a trade journal, business report or scientific journal.

It will therefore be seen that if patent protection is considered desirable, marketing or advertising of a new product or process must be delayed until a patent application is filed in at least one of the member states of the Paris Convention.

Definition of 'obvious'

Whilst the requirement that an invention must be new is an understandable and objective test, the requirement that an invention must also not be obvious is more problematical because what is not obvious to one person may be perfectly obvious to another. In practice, an invention is not considered to be obvious if it involves an 'inventive step' over and above the prior art, meaning a step taken by the inventor which would not ordinarily have occurred to others who are skilled in the technological art to which the invention relates. For some inventions, such as the hovercraft, it is easy to see where the inventive step lies, but difficulty arises when what may appear to be minor improvements are made to existing products.

'Improvements'

Perhaps surprisingly, the majority of all patents issued constitute improvements to existing products and processes, often only minor improvements which have, nevertheless, made the product or process better in some way or other.

To illustrate this point, consider the improvements which have been made to the humble office stapler since someone thought up the idea of a hand-operated device for automatically dispensing individual staples through two or more sheets of paper. The device incorporates an anvil plate on the reverse side of the paper which folds the free ends of the staple inwards when the upper arm is pressed downwards, thereby securing the paper together. Modern staplers now include such refinements as a rotatable anvil plate so that the staple can be selectively splayed outwards or inwards; a flexible plastic strip is now connected between the upper arm of the stapler and the spring-loaded carriage so that when the stapler is opened the carriage automatically slides backwards to allow easy insertion of fresh supplies of staples; and it is even possible to buy staplers with a blade attached to the side which can be used for removing unwanted staples from paper and for opening letters.

Many other minor modifications have been made to the basic design and construction of the office stapler and patents have been granted for these. It will be apparent that each and every minor improvement makes the stapler more saleable than its predecessor and hence it is not difficult to see why patents have been sought for each of them.

Exclusions from patentability

Over and above the requirement of novelty and inventiveness, there are certain other categories of inventions which are, nevertheless, still not considered to be worthy of patent protection. These include:

- discoveries, scientific theories or mathematical methods;
- literary, dramatic, musical or artistic works or any other aesthetic creations whatsoever;
- schemes, rules or methods for performing a mental act, playing a game or doing business, or programs for computers;
- inventions comprising the mere presentation of information;
- inventions the publication or exploitation of which would be generally expected to encourage offensive, immoral or antisocial behaviour; and

- any variety of animal or plant or any essentially biological process for the production of animals or plants, except micro-biological processes or products derived from such processes.

Despite the foregoing impressive list of exclusions, in practice most inventions which can find industrial applicability are found to be patentable, provided that they are new and not obvious. Even computer programs can form part of patentable subject matter if incorporated within an apparatus or process so that the combination results in a technical advance over the prior art. Thus, although it is not possible to obtain a patent for a computer program itself, it is possible to patent the application of a computer program within an apparatus or a process which results in a new and useful technical advance in the art to which it relates.

What the patent specification contains

Unlike the old Royal Letters Patent, which simply declared that the patentee had a right to do something or other to the exclusion of everyone else, the modern equivalent, the patent specification contains a comprehensive technical description of the invention and ends with a list of claims which define the legal scope of the patent. An example is shown in Appendix 1, which is in fairly typical form and begins with a preamble describing the background technical art to which the invention relates, followed by a brief description of what the invention is. There then follows a full technical description made with reference to the various drawings, which also form part of the patent specification. Finally, there is a set of legal claims defining the scope of the protection conferred by the patent and which distinguish the invention from the prior art.

Preparation of the patent specification

The preparation and submission of patent applications is a specialist art in itself and in the United Kingdom is usually only undertaken by qualified patent agents (now also called patent attorneys), most of whom belong to the Chartered Institute of Patent Agents. The skill and care necessary in preparing such a document cannot be overemphasized, and if an invention is worth patenting at all, it is worth employing professionally qualified people to handle the matter. This ensures that the invention has the best possible chance of being patented and, even more importantly, that the patent claims provide an adequate degree of protection from copying by also covering variations and modifications to the invention.

Cost

As will be seen from Chapter 13, the cost of applying for and obtaining the grant of a patent in just one country can be alarmingly high, particularly for inventions which by their nature are extremely technical and therefore require a greater amount of professional time and expertise to describe adequately and be distinguished from the prior art. A significant proportion of these costs, which include official filing fees, have to be met when the patent application is first filed at the Patent Office. Because of this, careful consideration should be given as to whether the anticipated commercial benefits in obtaining a patent justify the time and expense involved, particularly bearing in mind that it is impossible to predict at the outset whether or not a patent will eventually be granted for the invention.

Is it worth applying for?

Applying for a patent is rather like betting on a horse, you pay money without any certainty of being rewarded. Even if a patent is granted, there is no certainty that it will be commercially valuable and worth the effort and expense in obtaining it. This does not, of course, mean that patenting an invention should be dismissed as being too risky, since the benefits of obtaining a good patent which excludes competitors from utilizing the invention are obvious. This is particularly so in market conditions which are increasingly competitive and where, all other things being equal, only the very best companies are able to survive. A patent can give a company a distinct edge over its competitors, as will be apparent from the previous example of the office stapler.

It is possible for a business manager to make a decision on whether or not to seek patent protection by relying upon personal knowledge of the industry and a 'feel' for the likely success of the invention once it is marketed. However, a scientific approach to the decision-making process is likely to yield more consistent results and thereby reduce costs over time. The true cost of obtaining a patent is the summation of the bills paid and the time taken by company personnel involved in the project. Sometimes the latter can be kept to an absolute minimum by relying upon the expertise of the professional patent adviser, but more often than not technical input from a company and in particular the inventor is usually required throughout the patenting process, which can and often does last several years. It is therefore suggested that a three-stage approach be taken prior to coming to a decision on whether or not to seek a patent for an invention, as follows:

1. Having identified what is considered to be an invention, discuss with those involved in making the invention alternative ways of producing the same result, including various advantages and disadvantages for each.
2. Carry out a commercial analysis based upon the premiss that a patent will be granted for the invention and try to estimate the likely advantages to the company assuming competitors are excluded from utilizing the invention as a result of the existence of a patent for it.
3. If, after considering the first two steps, it is still considered worth while pursuing the project, obtain a preliminary opinion from a qualified patent agent to determine whether, assuming there is no closely relevant prior art which would prevent the grant of a worthwhile patent, the invention is likely to be patentable. The cost of seeking such an opinion is relatively modest and unlikely to exceed a few hundred pounds.

If the result of the foregoing steps indicates that the invention is technically and commercially worth while and theoretically patentable a decision can then be made with a certain measure of confidence on whether or not to proceed with the project.

Prior art searches

The level of confidence can be increased by also requesting the patent agent to carry out a search of the prior art before rendering a decision on the patentability of the invention. Prior art searches of this nature are discussed in more detail in Chapter 9 and have advantages as well as disadvantages. The disadvantages are the increased cost and the delay in obtaining the results of a search. It would be unusual for any comprehensive prior art search to be completed for under £1,000 and the time taken for the search could be several weeks, thus delaying the filing of the patent application and increasing the risk that a competitor may, in the intervening period, file a patent application covering essentially the same invention.

Thus, the accuracy of a preliminary opinion by a patent agent can therefore be improved with such a search but at the expense of delay and extra cost. On the other hand, money saved by not requesting a prior art search before a decision is made on whether to proceed with a patent application can go towards the cost of filing the patent application itself, which in most instances is likely to be around the £2–3,000 mark. Perhaps for this reason, most applicants choose to file first in the knowledge that the Patent Office will, if requested, carry out its own prior art search at some time during the early stages of the patent application and before any significant expenditure has been made.

Time span for an application

Unless an invention is particularly complex in technical terms a patent specification can usually be drawn up by a qualified patent agent within one or two weeks and then filed at the Patent Office. The procedure from then onwards is quite complicated but can be divided roughly into four stages spread over approximately three-and-a-half to four-and-a-half years. These are as follows:

1. Preliminary examination and search.
2. Publication of the patent application.
3. Substantive examination.
4. Grant or refusal of the patent application.

Each of these four stages include certain time limits by which particular things must be done or steps completed by either the applicant or the Patent Office, although variations in deadlines are sometimes permitted. Throughout these stages, the applicant has options either to proceed quickly or slowly and sometimes for cost considerations the latter route is chosen. However, as a general rule, the first stage is usually completed within a year of filing the application, publication of the patent application occurs around 18 months from filing, substantive examination is commenced at around the two-year mark and a decision on whether or not to grant a patent can usually be expected between the third and fourth year from filing. The decision must, in any event, be given within four-and-a-half years from the filing date or, if priority is claimed from an earlier patent filing in another country under the Paris Convention (discussed at the end of Chapter 1), within four-and-a-half years from that earlier filing date.

Stage 1

The first stage of preliminary examination and search is designed to get the patent application in order for publication, to be then followed after publication by substantive examination. Preliminary examination consists of checking the documents to see that the description, claims and drawings (if any) are in the proper form (i.e. generally similar to those shown in the patent specification of Appendix 1), that the various application forms have been filled out correctly and the correct fees paid.

The first stage also includes a search of the prior art by the Patent Office, which has to be requested and paid for by the applicant within a year from filing. The fees are not substantial and are considerably less than an applicant would expect to pay for a prior art search carried out by a patent agent before the filing of the application, but there are disadvantages. The first is that a prior art search by the Patent Office usually takes between four and six months to be completed. The second is that, perhaps because of manpower shortages at the Patent Office, it is sometimes the case that the search is not as thorough as it could be and relevant prior art is not located. Although this may appear to be an advantage to an applicant in that by not locating a relevant item of prior art the applicant then has a better chance of obtaining a patent, in reality this is not the case since it is standard practice for someone who is being sued for patent infringement to have an extensive search of the prior art carried out, usually leading to the discovery of all relevant prior art. As a consequence, if the Patent Office has missed prior art that it should have found, the defendant in a patent infringement action can counterclaim for revocation of the patent if the newly found prior art is the same as or closely similar to the patented invention. It will be apparent that in those circumstances all of the costs initially associated with obtaining the patent and then litigating it would have been wasted and, in most instances, an award of costs would also be made in favour of the defendant requiring the owner of the patent to reimburse the majority of his legal expenses.

All this means that, even if the original decision is to file a patent application without a prior art search, it is still useful to have one carried out independently of the Patent Office search within the first year, so that all relevant information is known to an applicant at a point in time when expenses are unlikely to be significant. It must also be borne in mind that if patent applications are going to be filed abroad then these must be filed within the first 12 months of the original filing date and, since costs are then multiplied by the number of countries for which patent protection is desired, it makes sense to have an independent prior art search carried out well before the end of the 12-month deadline and before decisions have to be made for filing foreign applications claiming priority from the original filing in the United Kingdom.

Stage 2

Once the preliminary examination and search is over – about 15 months after the original filing – the application is forwarded to the government printer, who then publishes a number of copies of the patent application at around the 18-month mark. These published patent specifications are very similar in format to the granted patent shown in Appendix 1 and are available to the public for purchase. Copies are also dispatched to several libraries within the United Kingdom and many patent offices around the world for the purpose of providing them with a continued update of new technology.

Since details of the invention are made available to the public before any decision is made on whether or not to grant a patent there is thus the risk that, having done so, a patent is refused and valuable technical information may then have been given away free to a competitor. Whilst this procedure may seem rather unfair, it is adopted by most countries who have patent examination systems, with the notable exception of the United States.

Patent applications in the United States remain secret and details of an invention are only published if a patent is granted. This is good for the applicant but bad for the public, particularly if there has been a long delay in obtaining a patent. The sudden appearance of a patent covering technology which is already in widespread use can cause severe problems, as can be illustrated by a patent which issued in 1976 from an original application filed in 1958 by an American inventor. The invention concerned a type of optically pumped laser which was in widespread use in industry during the 1960s and early 1970s. Grant of the patent had been delayed because the application conflicted with another one which had been filed at about the same time for closely similar technology. Evidence of who was first to invent had to be adduced, there were several hearings in the US Patent Office and an appeal to the US Courts, which eventually ended in a ruling that the patent should be issued. The problem was that the industry had by then been using the laser for many years and was suddenly faced with the prospect of having to pay royalties for the duration of the patent, which is 17 years in the United States. It has been observed that although the owner of the patent was not responsible for the delay in its issuance, nevertheless the value of the patent was artificially much higher than it would otherwise have been if it had been issued at a stage when the industry was in its infancy.

In contrast, publication of a patent application at a relatively early stage serves to advise the public as to what an applicant seeks to patent, which acts as a warning and also provides an opportunity for third parties to submit prior art they are aware of to the Patent Office for consideration by the examiner. Such additional prior art can be lodged at any time after publication and up to the grant of the patent.

Stage 3

Once a patent application has been published, it is necessary to request what is called 'substantive examination' within six months, this being the examination to determine whether a patent should be granted or refused. There is a fee for requesting this examination and if it is not paid on time the application automatically lapses.

Substantive examination is carried out by a technically qualified examiner at the Patent Office, of which there are many. The examiners are split into various groups depending on the area of technology concerned so that each examiner is usually familiar with the background technology concerning inventions which fall within his group. Thus, a patent for a new inorganic chemical compound will be examined by one of several examiners assigned to deal with patents relating to inorganic chemistry and, similarly, a patent application for a mechanical invention such as a new tin-opener will be assigned to an examiner used to dealing with mechanical inventions of that type.

Each examiner must carefully review the various items of prior art found in the search and compare them with the subject matter of the invention as described in the claims accompanying the patent application. Usually, the examiner will adopt a defensive stance and will initially refuse an application, citing a variety of reasons, such as prior disclosure of the same inventive concept in one or more of the prior art documents relied upon. Thus, the first official letter received from the Patent Office during substantive examination (often referred to as the first 'official action'), usually brings with it a rejection or request for amendment and there then follows an exchange of correspondence between the examiner and the patent agent used by the applicant. The patent agent's job is wherever possible to counter arguments raised by the examiner with a detailed analysis of the prior art to try to distinguish it from the invention; this often entails narrowing the scope of the claims of the patent application, thus making them more easily distinguished over the prior art.

In general, patent applications are usually filed with claims which are optimistically wide and as examination proceeds they are narrowed to a sufficient extent so as to be clearly distinguished from the prior art. The problem, of course, is that if they are made too narrow then although the invention itself may still be covered by the claims, variations on the invention may not, thus making it easy for competitors to design around the invention to achieve the same technical result. Although this tactic does not always work, the possibility of it happening is one reason why the services of qualified patent agents are essential in order to obtain worthwhile patent protection.

Stage 4

After an exchange of correspondence between the examiner and the patent agent a decision will then be made on whether to refuse or grant a patent in respect of the, usually, amended claims. In practice well over half of all patent applications are granted although there is wide disparity between their respective values in commercial terms.

The patent is granted in the form as shown in Appendix 1 and lasts for a maximum of 20 years from the filing date. This is not a fixed term and the patent has to be continually kept in force by payment of renewal fees at yearly intervals. Initially, these fees are relatively modest but increase significantly towards the end of the patent term, making it probable that only the most valuable patents are kept in force by their owners for the entire 20-year period.

Many of the full-term patents relate to pharmaceutical products which have had to undergo many years of field trials before being cleared for use. For these products, it is now possible to obtain a supplementary protection certificate (SPC) from the Patent Office if an application is made before the patent expires. An SPC confers the same kind of protection on the product as a patent including the right to sue for infringement. The maximum duration of an SPC is five years but the length of term granted by the Patent Office depends on how long it took for marketing authorization to be obtained for the drug.

Conclusion

It will therefore been seen that obtaining a patent is laborious and time consuming, hence the need for a careful assessment at regular intervals of the merits of proceeding with the application. In particular, if it is found subsequent to filing a patent application that prior art exists which is so generally similar to the invention that broad patent rights are not available, it is prudent to again carry out the initial evaluative steps referred to earlier in this chapter to determine if it is still worth while continuing, or if it would be better to cut losses and abandon the application. This is particularly so prior to the publication of the application where, if it is withdrawn before preparations for publication have been completed (at around 15 months from filing), the invention will not be published and hence competitors will not be given full details of it for free.

Alternative procedures

Although the procedures described above relate only to patent applications filed in accordance with the procedure laid down by the UK Patents Act 1977, there are two other ways of obtaining a UK patent which deserve mention. One is by means of an application filed under the Patent Cooperation Treaty (a so-called 'PCT' application), which is again an international treaty to which 58 countries now belong and which initially only requires the filing of a single application in one member state. A single unified examination including a prior art search is then carried out by a central receiving office in Switzerland administered by the World Intellectual Property Organization (WIPO). This search is then usually considered to be sufficient for the purposes of national requirements. A favourable examination report from WIPO is often enough to convince a national examiner that the invention is patentable and the application is then granted in the normal way in each member state upon payment of national filing fees.

The primary advantage of filing a PCT application, as opposed to a number of national applications in countries where patent protection is required, lies in the fact that the initial fees are significantly lower than would otherwise be the case if individual patent applications were filed in all countries of interest. The total fees are in fact a little higher but most do not have to be paid until about 25–30 months from the original filing date, thus effectively delaying significant expenditure when the worth of a patent may still have to be fully evaluated. The disadvantage lies in the possibility of receiving an unfavourable report from WIPO – which then has a knock-on effect (akin to putting all eggs in one basket and then dropping it) – rather than allowing individual Patent Office examiners in each country to assess the merits of the invention for themselves.

The other way of obtaining patent rights which are effective in the United Kingdom is through the European Patent Convention, as mentioned briefly at the beginning of this chapter. The procedure is very similar to a national patent application filed in the UK, and in fact a European patent application can be filed either in Munich, The Hague or at the Patent Office in Newport. The advantage of filing a European patent application is that it tends to save costs, particularly in the early stages, but the disadvantage is that once again all eggs are in the same basket.

The European Patent Convention differs from the Patent Cooperation Treaty in carrying out a full examination of a patent application and, if it is successful, granting the patent. Once granted, the patent effectively reverts to a bundle of national patents in those states designated on the application form.

3 Trade marks and how to register them

The function and use of trade marks

Trade marks were invented in order to identify a particular manufacturer and distinguish his products from those of others. The earliest known use occurred in pre-Roman times when it became common for potters to put their name on each item of pottery for identification purposes when sharing kilns. Nowadays, the function of a trade mark is much more diverse and in its broadest sense is used not just by the trade mark owner but by the trade and public to identify the quality of product rather than who has actually manufactured it. Trade marks are also used to distinguish the origin and quality of services offered to the trade and public, such as financial services offered by a bank.

A trade mark can be almost anything which is used to distinguish goods or services offered by one party from those of another. Terms such as house mark, trade name, brand name, logo, etc., usually only mean a unique business identifier which is used for distinguishing the goods or services offered by the owner from those of others. Anything which does this is by its nature a trade mark, but not all trade marks qualify for registration.

A trade mark can be sold or licensed for others to use for a royalty fee and can also be registered, although it does not have to be, as will be explained in this chapter.

Counterfeiting

In some countries counterfeiting at the expense of the legitimate trade mark owner overseas is considered normal trade practice, particularly by those governments which have a vested interest in ensuring that foreign currency is earned. Such countries are usually, although not exclusively, those which make it difficult for foreigners to register their marks whilst making it relatively simple for their nationals to use and register the marks in preference to the legitimate trade mark owner. Fortunately, most of the important trading nations do not fall within this category and have developed laws which are designed to protect the genuine trade mark owner from unfair copying or exploitation, whether deliberate or unintentional. Unintentional copying can arise simply by virtue of an ill-advised choice of a new trade mark which is later found to be too similar to an already established mark, so that confusion or deception of the trade or public occurs. In those circumstances, the owner of the first mark usually has an understandable grievance and will take action through the Courts to prevent further use of the later mark.

Legal redress

Chapter 1 referred to the two legal systems operating in tandem in the United Kingdom, the statute law and the common law. Each system recognizes trade mark rights and therefore each has to be considered whenever disputes arise. Many other countries adopt the same type of system based upon English law and these countries can roughly be categorized into all former British Commonwealth countries, Ireland and the United States. Most European countries adopt a rather different approach in only recognizing trade mark rights as a result of registration but at the same time also recognizing as a general principle that unfair competition should not be allowed. In essence, each system achieves the same objective.

Other countries have legal systems which, as explained, often appear to be deliberately designed to make it difficult for foreigners to acquire and assert what would be regarded elsewhere as legitimate trade mark rights. As a general rule, these countries do not recognize trade mark rights at all unless the trade mark in question is registered and, again, little or no effort is made to determine whether the person seeking registration owns the mark.

The importance of registering a trade mark

Since it follows that in many countries common law or similar rights exist to protect the interests of legitimate trade mark owners, what then is the point of registering a trade mark in such countries? The answer lies in the different nature of the legal rights conferred and the steps which have to be taken in order to assert such rights against third-party infringers. Under the common law, as is discussed further in Chapter 8, it is possible for the owner of an unregistered trade mark to take action to prevent use of the mark, or a similar mark, on the same or similar goods or services if, but only if, the owner can establish by way of factual evidence that he has a reputation in the mark and the defendant is guilty of making, however innocently, a misrepresentation in the course of trade which is calculated to deceive or cause confusion and which actually does so, or is likely to do so. Whether this is established to the satisfaction of the Court depends very much upon the facts of each case and accordingly there is an in-built uncertainty which depends upon the quality of the evidence offered to the Court. The plaintiff must show as a prerequisite that he has a reputation in respect of his mark and having done so, usually by way of presenting market survey evidence, it is then necessary to try to establish by way of evidence the likelihood of the trade or public being confused to a material degree.

It is therefore clear that the owner of a relatively new mark who suddenly finds that someone else has adopted the same mark, or one which is considered confusingly similar to it, may not be able to take action to prevent the use of the second mark because of lack of sufficient reputation or evidence of confusion. Additionally, the legal costs in taking action under the common law are usually very high in view of the high standard of factual evidence required by the Court. For these and other reasons, a system of registration was first adopted in the last century which has made it far cheaper and much more certain for trade mark owners to acquire and enforce trade mark rights.

Rights acquired by registering a trade mark

By registering a trade mark, the owner acquires a monopoly in the use of the mark which can be used to prevent others from using identical or similar marks in respect of those goods or services for which the mark is registered. Registration also makes it difficult, if not impossible, for third parties to register similar marks for similar goods and services, since the Trade Marks Registry will not normally permit closely similar or even identical marks to be registered in respect of closely similar goods or services. Thus, registration of a trade mark constitutes a neat and simple way of establishing rights and if a dispute arises it is therefore much easier to assert those rights against the defendant in Court. The mark is either registered or not, and if the use complained of is in respect of the same goods or services then the judge simply has to decide whether the respective marks are confusingly similar. If the answer is yes, then that is the end of the matter and the defendant has to stop using his mark.

Another advantage of the registration system is that it is of public record and anyone can search to see which marks have been registered and which have not. It is therefore possible for a marketing manager who proposes to adopt a new trade mark to carry out searches beforehand in order to ensure that no one else has already registered the same or a similar mark, thus making it more certain, but never absolutely so, that disputes will not arise after the often expensive exercise of launching a new product or service under a new trade mark has commenced.

Unregistrable and registrable marks

That not all trade marks are registrable simply reflects the fact that some businesses choose to adopt trade marks which are very descriptive of the type of product or service, its quality or geographical origin. Such marks are inherently unregistrable. The rationale in refusing registration of such marks lies in the fact that registration endows a monopoly in the use of the mark. It cannot be right for one party to obtain registration of a descriptive or highly suggestive word that other traders would legitimately want to use. This does not mean that such marks cannot continue to be used as trade marks by those who adopt them, but just that registration can in most instances never be obtained and common law rights have to be relied upon instead. Marks which the Courts have ruled to be fundamentally unregistrable include YORK for lorry trailers, because it is a well-known geographical place where lorry trailers could be manufactured, PERFECTION for soap, because it is entirely laudatory and WELDMESH because it is entirely descriptive of steel wire mesh.

Marks which are inherently registrable are those which are considered to be distinctive in law, as opposed to simply being distinctive in fact. Distinctive marks are those which do not describe a character or quality of goods or services and are not otherwise prohibited, such as marks suggesting royal patronage and the like. Marks which are inherently registrable include KODAK, a meaningless invented word and WHITE HORSE for whisky, since although the mark has a well-known meaning, it does not describe in any way the nature or quality of the product.

In between these two extremes are marks which may have some element of distinctiveness about them, but which also include some element of descriptiveness. These marks can still be registered but it is sometimes difficult to obtain registration unless the mark has been used for several years and has become distinctive through such use.

Conclusion

It will be seen from these brief considerations that, as with obtaining a patent, registering a trade mark is not always straightforward and often requires effort and thus expense, although usually not to the same level as with patents.

Choosing and registering a trade mark

Pitfalls for managers

When choosing a trade mark, the business manager is faced with a dilemma, although this is often not apparent at the outset. The dilemma arises because marketing considerations usually require that a trade mark for a new product or service should help to sell the product or service by suggesting superiority over rival products and services, or at least by suggesting the type of product or service on which the mark is used. This immediately conflicts with the basic requirement that to be registrable a mark must in some way be distinctive and therefore not descriptive. Thus, marks which are easily registrable are often not favoured by marketing personnel, whose priority is to maximize the sale of the product or service rather than to worry about whether or not the chosen mark is registrable. The problem with this approach, however, is that it tends to have only short-term benefits which, over time, may prove to be more burdensome than adopting a mark which is easily registrable, and thus easily protected from copying. As a general rule, the more descriptive or suggestive a mark is the harder it is to protect from imitation, whether or not the mark is registrable. Conversely, the more distinctive a mark is the easier it is to protect both at common law and by means of registration, and thus the easier it is to retain a reputation in the mark once it has become established.

Choosing a trade mark

No one would argue that the mark KODAK was in the least descriptive or suggestive of the character or quality of the goods on which the mark was used when it was first adopted. It is a highly distinctive but meaningless word which in marketing terms has now come full circle to denote state-of-the-art photographic and related products of excellent quality. As such, the mark has achieved an enviable position in the photographic industry and, without exaggeration, is the single most valuable asset of the Eastman Kodak Company. A mark which is fundamentally flawed in terms of registrability almost never achieves such a status, can often never be registered and may even suffer the ultimate indignity of being copied at will by enterprising third parties.

At this point it would be useful to review the results of some of the applications to register trade marks by a variety of businesses in the United Kingdom from the mid-1980s to date (see Table 3.1). It will be apparent from the table that the initial choice of a trade mark should be based upon a combination of factors additional to marketing considerations. This does not mean, of course, that only registrable trade marks should be adopted

Table 3.1 Results of some recent applications to register trade marks in the United Kingdom

Trademark	Goods/services	Decision
SURETY	Glass and glass products for architectural and building purposes	Registration refused since the mark was considered descriptive and laudatory
ALWAYS	Non-woven goods, perfumes, cosmetics, soaps, sanitary preparations	Registration refused, the mark being descriptive and not-distinctive of the goods and as such should be left free for other traders to use
BIO-PROBE	Disposable flow probes for blood pumps	Registration refused as the mark was considered not to be an invented word but descriptive of the goods
CRACKLE	Breakfast cereals	Registration refused since other traders in the same goods should be free to use the word CRACKLE
A device mark composed of a picture of one man wrapping a blanket around another man in flames	Fire blankets and clothing for protection against fire	Registration refused since the mark was considered to be pictorially descriptive of the goods
BRETON	Machines	Registration refused since BRETON is a common surname and is also a geographical area in north-west France and as such would be descriptive of goods of BRETON origin, or deceptive if they were not
BETA	Video recorders and cassettes	Registration refused since the mark was considered to be generic at the date of application as being the name of the goods
FRANKWURST	Sausages	Registration refused since the mark was considered to be a mere combination of the surname FRANK and the German word WURST meaning a large sausage
AFRICAR	Vehicles	Registration refused since the mark was considered to be phonetically identical to the geographical name Africa and was therefore considered to be not an invented word and not distinctive
ORGASM	Cosmetics	This time registration was refused because the mark was not only considered to be not distinctive but also the word 'ORGASM' was likely to offend many people
SPARK	Terminals for electrical apparatus, instruments and installations	Registration refused because although the word SPARK by itself was not directly descriptive, its use with other words such as 'SPARK FREE' or 'SPARK RESISTANT' would directly describe important characteristics of the goods and the word SPARK is also one which other traders would be likely to wish to use without any improper motive
ROYAL MAIL	Wrapping paper, printed matter, stationery, stamps and albums, all relating to postal services	Registration refused because the mark was considered to be descriptive and not distinctive

Table 3.1—continued

Trademark	Goods/services	Decision
ANGELA CUMMINGS	Cutlery, forks and spoons	In the absence of evidence of acquired distinctiveness through use, the mark was considered to be not distinctive, being composed of a common forename and a common surname
BUDGET	All services connected with the renting and leasing of vehicles	Registration was refused because although the mark had been used on a substantial scale it was held that the mark was inherently not distinctive and was a word which might well be used in promotional materials by other traders and was commonly used in advertising of all kinds including those relating to vehicle hire services
DAKOTA	Beer	Registration refused in view of the overwhelming geographical significance of the mark
COOLPAK	Insulated containers	Registration refused because 'cool' plus the phonetic equivalent of 'pack' was directly descriptive of the goods
SOFTWARE 2000	Computer programs	Registration refused because 'software' was not an invented word and had a direct reference to the character of the goods, numerals were notoriously not distinctive because of their common use by traders in advertising and, in particular, 2000 indicated the year 2000, implying that the goods were of the latest and most advanced type
FLUSHAWAY	Disposable medical products	Registration refused since the mark was directly descriptive of goods which could be flushed away

and used since registration in the United Kingdom is not crucial, only preferable. Given the choice between a highly descriptive trade mark which is unregistrable but very desirable from a marketing standpoint, as opposed to a highly distinctive, registrable but much less attractive mark, the choice will always be the former rather than the latter. However, if there are two marks to choose from and one is only slightly less desirable from a marketing standpoint but is more readily registrable, adoption of that mark is likely to prove more beneficial in the long term.

Using professional advice

This suggests that advice needs to be taken at an early stage and before a trade mark has been chosen in order to determine whether or not it is likely to be registrable. Advice of this nature can be obtained from registered trade mark agents, of which there are several hundred in the United Kingdom. Although anyone can act as an agent for someone else in securing trade mark registration, and even offer advice in connection with registrability, generally speaking only those on the Register of Trade Mark Agents are professionally qualified to do so, in much the same way as are chartered patent agents who give advice concerning patents.

Using a registered trade mark agent at an early stage can avoid the embarrassment and expense of a dispute arising out of the adoption of a trade mark which is considered to be confusingly similar to someone else's. In particular, a registered trade mark agent will be able to advise on whether or not anyone else has already registered, or applied to register, the same mark or a similar one in respect of the same or similar goods or services. If the answer is no and the mark is considered to be registrable an application can be made to register it. However, it should be noted that because it is not mandatory to register marks in the United Kingdom there is always the risk that the chosen mark may already be in use by a third party, who might at a later date dispute any application to register the same or a similar mark and could even take action under the common law to prevent acts of passing off. Thus, in the initial stages at least, it is never possible to be absolutely certain as to whether or not the adoption of a new mark will be objected to. On the other hand, steps can be taken to ensure that the risk of objection is kept to a minimum by carrying out clearance searches and obtaining professional advice, as discussed further in Chapter 9.

Obtaining a trade mark registration

The registration process is in many respects similar to that for obtaining a patent but the stages occur in a slightly different sequence. These stages are as follows:

1. Preliminary examination and search.
2. Substantive examination.
3. Publication of accepted trade mark applications to allow third parties the opportunity to oppose registration.
4. Registration of the trade mark if no successful opposition is filed.

Before describing the procedures involved in registering a trade mark it is necessary to consider several ground rules which may not be entirely obvious at first sight. The first of these is that it is not possible to secure registration of a trade mark for all goods and services. When applying for registration it is necessary to be specific as to which particular goods or services are to be the subject of registration. Thus, it can and often does happen that the same or closely similar trade marks are registered by different parties, provided that the goods or services covered by the registrations do not overlap and are not so similar as to make people wonder whether the goods or services emanate from the same source.

To illustrate by way of specific example, the mark SMITHS is quite happily shared between, on the one hand, a potato crisp manufacturer, and on the other a manufacturer of electrical automotive components. This principle of shared marks cannot, however, be considered as an invitation for one party freely to adopt the trade mark of another in respect of different goods since other considerations such as the risk of passing off under the common law may prevent this, particularly where the trade mark in question is highly distinctive and is widely known to be the mark of only one party. Again, the mark KODAK is likely to fall into this category of marks which are probably unavailable for use by any party other than the Eastman Kodak Company. Other examples include GUCCI, ROLEX, CARTIER, ROLLS-ROYCE and COCA COLA.

A second factor which stems from the first is that all goods and services for which registration may be obtained are grouped into various classes ranging from 1 to 42. Appendix 2 lists those classes and gives a general indication as to which goods or services are found in each. Goods are covered by class 1 to 34, whereas services can be found in classes 35 to 42. Class 1 generally covers industrial chemicals and similar products, class 5 covers pharmaceutical products, class 12 covers vehicles including aeroplanes and ships, class 25 covers clothing, classes 29 and 30 each cover various kinds of foodstuffs and so on. Similarly, class 35 covers advertising and business services, such as accountancy, employment agencies, management consultancy and television advertising. Similar specific services can be found in classes 36 to 41, with class 42 being mostly reserved for miscellaneous services not found in other classes.

Considerations when filing an application

When filing a trade mark application in the United Kingdom it is therefore necessary to identify the particular class of goods or services of interest and the specific goods or services falling within that class for which registration is being sought. This system makes the examiner's job of searching for conflicting marks very much easier than it otherwise would be since confusion between two marks can arise in a variety of different ways, not simply when the marks are spelt similarly or, if the applied-for mark is of a pictorial nature, when the message conveyed by it is broadly similar to another mark. Phonetic similarities are also relevant, as is the doctrine of 'imperfect recollection', whereby it is recognized that human memory is not always consistent and an imperfectly recollected mark known to be that of one trader may become confused with another mark owned by someone else.

To illustrate by way of example, the owners of the trade mark ARISTOC were successful in preventing the use of the trade mark RYSTA on the same range of goods, i.e. women's stockings. They successfully argued in Court that RYSTA would normally be pronounced RISSTA making it phonetically similar to ARISTOC. This case was perhaps an extreme example but it illustrates two points, the first being that the old saying that at the end of the day the judge decides, is perfectly true. The second is that it is dangerous simply to compare trade marks for confusing similarity side-by-side where detailed differences become more apparent and can thus lead to a false assumption that a dispute will not arise.

All of these considerations have to be borne in mind not only by those persons seeking registration of trade marks and their legal advisers, but also by the Trade Marks Registry examination staff who have the job of identifying previously registered or applied for trade marks which are or could be confusingly similar with an applied-for mark. In practice, the Registry usually err on the side of caution and will raise an objection based upon a previously registered or applied-for mark even where only relatively slight similarities exist. This is not a particularly bad philosophy to adopt but it does mean that detailed and compelling arguments have to be submitted to the Registry in most cases in order to overcome objections of this nature. In turn, this means that recourse should be had to the services of registered trademark agents who are familiar with the kind of arguments that will succeed.

The Trade Marks Register

The Trade Marks Register itself is split into two parts, Part A being reserved for those marks which are considered to be inherently distinctive or for those marks which, whilst not initially being so, have nevertheless become distinctive through substantial use in the United Kingdom, usually over a period of at least five years. Part B of the Register is reserved for those marks which whilst not being inherently distinctive are nevertheless considered capable of distinguishing one trader's products or services from those of another. Part A marks include invented words and words or phrases having no direct reference to the character or quality of the goods or services offered. On the other hand, Part B marks are usually more descriptive or suggestive of the goods or services, although not entirely so, otherwise they would not be registrable at all.

Theoretically, a Part A mark is intended to provide greater rights to the trade mark owner than a Part B mark and there are certain other advantages in obtaining registration in Part A as opposed to Part B. However, as regards the extent of protection available in practical terms there is little difference between the two, as is discussed in greater detail in Chapter 7.

The registration procedure

The registration procedure begins with an application filed at the Trade Marks Registry, which is now located in Newport. Applications are still accepted for filing purposes in London but they are then transferred for examination to the Newport Registry. The application form must identify the applicant, the mark, the part of the Register for which application is being made (usually all applications are filed in Part A initially) and the particular range of goods or services for which registration is sought.

Invalid applications

An important point to note is that the applicant must at the date of filing either be using the mark or have a firm and present intention to use it, otherwise the application is considered invalidly made. The only exception to this general rule is that if the applicant does not use or intend to use, then it can instead at the date of filing simultaneously apply to record another user of the mark (termed a 'registered user'), which in ordinary commercial terms can simply be considered as a licensee. Thus, care should be taken to ensure that where, for example, a non-trading holding company is the applicant, the trade mark application is accompanied by an application to record a registered user, otherwise the application will be invalid.

Preliminary examination and search

Once received at the Registry, the trade mark application undergoes a preliminary examination to determine that the documents are in order and that no mistakes have been made on the application form. A search is then carried out to determine if there are any trade marks already registered or applied for in the same class or related classes containing similar goods or services. If there are, details of all marks located are put on the file.

Substantive examination

The file is then transferred to an examiner who must consider a variety of points prior to issuing the first examination report. These include whether or not the mark is at all descriptive or suggestive of the goods or services. If so, the application may be rejected outright, or an offer may be made to transfer the mark for Part B registration. An alternative would be to invite the applicant to prove that although the mark is prima facie indistinctive, nevertheless through use over a number of years it has become distinctive. If a mark consists of a geographical place name or a surname it will usually be rejected and if the geographical place name is well-known, such as YORK, in most cases it will be considered as being fundamentally unregistrable no matter how much evidence of prior use there has been. Marks which are entirely laudatory also fall into this category of being fundamentally unregistrable, for example, words like PERFECTION.

There are also marks which include matter which is excluded from registration by virtue of international treaties. Thus, it is not possible to register marks which include a red cross on a white background, national flags, the Olympic symbol, abbreviations such as ANZAC and so on. There are many other potential objections which can be raised to a trade mark application but it is beyond the scope of this book to deal with them all. However, it will be apparent that the examination procedure is quite complex and hence time consuming, taking around a year from filing before the first examination report can be expected. The good news is that if the mark is considered to be registrable then when it is eventually registered the rights conferred by registration date back to the filing date.

Limitations and conditions after registration

Sometimes a mark is accepted for registration subject to certain limitations and conditions which are usually designed to minimize possible deception of the trade or public when a trade mark is actually in use. For example, if a particular mark indicates that the goods or services supplied come from a particular location then a condition of registration will be imposed to the effect that, in use, the mark must only be used in respect of goods or services originating from that geographical location. If the trade mark owner does not observe the conditions of use then this constitutes a ground for revoking the registration.

A condition limiting the rights of the trade mark owner is often necessary when the mark in question contains words or phrases which other traders should be free to use. The mark as a whole may be considered registrable but subject to a condition disclaiming exclusive rights to use of the descriptive or suggestive part. Examples are shown in Appendix 2, which is an extract from the weekly *Trade Marks Journal* published by the Trade Marks Registry. The mark PRINCESS HOUSE is proposed to be registered in class 28 in respect of games, play things and similar goods. The mark carries with it a disclaimer to exclusive rights in the word 'HOUSE'. Thus, once the mark is registered, the owner cannot use the fact of registration to prevent third parties from using the word HOUSE in other marks, although this does not, of course, mean that third parties can use the rest of the mark.

Similarly, the owners of FLOO MAN CHOO have no exclusive rights to the word MAN. The other mark advertised with such a disclaimer condition (Application No. 1424109) is interesting because this time the disclaimer condition is not absolute, although this may not be apparent at first glance. The disclaimer is only to the exclusive use of 'a letter "C"', meaning that the applicant is entitled to exclusive use of the particular form of the letter 'C' used in the mark.

The final mark shown, ROY'S and device is indicated as having been 'Advertised before acceptance'. This means that the Trade Mark Registry has reserved judgement on registrability of the mark until third parties have been given a chance to oppose it, thus permitting the Registry to refuse registration regardless of any opposition by a third party. Usually, this is where a mark was originally unregistrable but the applicant has been able to show that through use over at least several years it has nevertheless acquired a degree of distinctiveness and therefore become registrable.

Publication of the accepted application

Unless a mark is hopelessly descriptive or laudatory it will normally be acceptable for registration, even if only after having been proven to be distinctive through use over many years. Once accepted for registration by the Trade Marks Registry then, as shown in Appendix 2, the mark is advertised in the *Trade Marks Journal* in order to allow third parties the opportunity to oppose the registration. In most instances opposition is not raised within the statutory one-month period for doing so and, upon the payment of a registration fee, the mark becomes registered. A registration certificate is then issued to the trade mark owner of the form shown in Appendix 3, which gives details of the mark, the goods or services for which it is registered and since when.

In those instances where a third party objects to registration it is necessary to formally oppose registration by filing a Notice of Opposition including supporting grounds, which are rather similar to pleadings in High Court litigation. The applicant is then given the opportunity to withdraw the application or defend it and, if the latter, a counter-statement has to be filed giving reasons why the applicant feels the mark should be registered. Evidence by both sides is then submitted to the Registry, culminating in a formal hearing where a senior examiner will decide whether or not to permit registration. Perhaps surprisingly, the results of a trade mark opposition hearing can be appealed to the Courts, even all the way up to the House of Lords if a point of law has to be decided.

Table 3.2 How decisions are arrived at when comparing one mark with another

Mark	Goods/services	Decision
LABOPHOT	Microscopes	The opponents owned a registration for LABOVIAL for the same goods but the respective marks were considered to be sufficiently different and the opposition failed
NOEVIR	Non-medicated toilet preparations	The owners of the mark NIVEA opposed on the grounds of confusing similarity but the opposition failed, it being held that the marks were sufficiently different such that no confusion was likely
BLACKGOLD	Garden composts	The owners of BROWNGOLD for the same goods succeeded in their opposition, it being held that the respective marks were confusingly similar
PROPAIN	Pharmaceuticals	The owners of the mark PROPEN succeeded in their opposition, again because of the possibility of confusion. It should be noted in particular that with respect to pharmaceuticals where there is a public safety factor the Trade Marks Registry or the Courts will usually err on the side of caution and refuse registration even if there is only a slight possibility of confusion
CANDIDE	Clothing for women	The owner of the mark CANDA could not prevent registration of CANDIDE, it being held that no confusion was likely
CANDIES	Footwear	The same opponent was this time successful because the respective marks were considered confusingly similar and the goods very close
CHELSEA MAN	Men's and boys' clothing	The owners of CHELSEA GIRL were unsuccessful in their opposition, there being no reasonable likelihood of deception and confusion
HYPOL	Building materials	An opposition by the owners of HYPOXAL succeeded, the marks being considered confusingly similar
SUPERSEAL	Draught excluders	The opponents did not rely upon any trade mark rights but successfully argued that the word SUPERSEAL was directly descriptive and given the laudatory significance of 'super' and common trade use of 'seal' the mark was refused registration
KOMPASS	Information services	The owners of the exclusive franchise for the same mark registered for printed publications were successful in their opposition, it being held that a substantial part of the market would associate KOMPASS directories with the opponent. This was a very interesting case because the applicant was Kompass International AG, the franchisor and owner of the mark KOMPASS for publications

Again, a review of opposition decisions handed down since 1985 is useful in indicating how they are arrived at when comparing one mark with another, (see Table 3.2).

Renewal of the registration

Assuming no opposition is filed and the mark is registered, the registration lasts for 7 years from the original filing date and can be renewed for successive periods of 14 years each upon the payment of a fairly modest renewal fee. In the United Kingdom the first mark ever registered was the famous BASS & TRIANGLE device which was registered in 1875 and is still registered, having been renewed no less than 11 times!

Trade marks can last forever but, as is explained later in this book, if they are to remain enforceable they must be looked after.

4 Registered designs

Patents provide protection for improvements made to products or processes, or the way in which they operate. A design registration does not protect the manner in which a product or process works, but the external appearance of an article of manufacture, such as a newly shaped teapot, or an existing product to which a new pattern has been applied. Designs of this nature are usually registrable if they appeal to the eye and are not solely functional. Put another way, a design will usually be registrable if it constitutes something which is considered aesthetically pleasing to the observer, the observer being a person who would ordinarily purchase such products.

The relevant law

The law relating to registered designs has changed over the last few years as a result of the Copyright, Designs and Patents Act 1988. The new Act has redefined what is meant as a registrable design and provides additional exclusions from registrability which were not present previously; depending upon when a design was registered, different considerations will now apply. The most significant of these is that designs are now registrable for up to 25 years whereas previously the maximum term was 15 years from the date of filing. Also important is the new exclusion from registrability of designs which are dependent upon the appearance of another article to which it is intended to form an integral part. For example, excluded from registrability are designs such as vehicle body panels and similar components which must fit or must match with part or all of the rest of the vehicle. The exclusion is obviously designed to ensure that customers who purchase products such as vehicles are free to decide for themselves whether or not to purchase 'genuine' spare parts manufactured by the original equipment manufacturer, or to shop around for usually less expensive parts which will nevertheless fit or match and do the same job.

Qualifications for registration

There is no hard and fast rule as to which products could be the subject of a registrable design, except that a qualifying product must be capable of being made and sold separately and the features of the design must be outwardly visible prior to a customer making a purchase. Thus, it is possible to register the design of a chocolate egg having a distinctive pattern on its outer shell, but if the pattern is on the inside of the shell it is not registrable. Similarly, it is not possible to register a new design of the external appearance of a house because it is not regarded as being an article of manufacture, having been constructed on site using a variety of building materials. On the other hand, the external appearance of a prefabricated building can and has been the subject of design registration because the entire building is manufactured first and only assembled on site afterwards.

The importance of an accurate description

There are two important points which must be understood about the registration of designs, the first being that a design is only registered in respect of a particular article or a set of articles normally sold as such, for example, a dinner service having the same pattern on each item of the set. Thus, the registration of a design consisting of a new pattern affixed to the side of a teapot would not be infringed by the use of the same pattern placed on the side of, say, a table lamp. This can cause difficulties, particularly where there is some argument as to the proper description to be given to an article incorporating the design, and it will be apparent that a poorly worded statement of what the article is may end up providing an unscrupulous competitor with an opportunity to take unfair advantage. To illustrate this, if the article is a newly designed plastic racing car it could quite properly be described as a 'toy vehicle' rather than 'plastic racing car' so that other vehicles of a similar design, not necessarily made of plastic, would be covered by the registration. Similarly, it is not necessary to describe a new pattern as being a 'pattern applied to the side of a teapot' when, instead, the statement describing the article could specify that the design in accordance with the registration is to be applied to a pot with a handle and spout, thereby also covering use of the pattern on a coffee pot as well. Although copyright laws can assist in most cases, nevertheless the advantage of obtaining design registration may be lost or unnecessarily restricted by a poor choice of statement as to what the article consists of.

The second important point is that as well as having to specify the article to which the design applies, an applicant must also specify the features of the design which are to be covered by the registration.

Designs are registrable in respect of articles having a new shape or configuration, pattern or ornament and it is necessary to specify which is applicable. In practice, shape and configuration are considered as being synonymous, and pattern and ornament are also. Thus, the maker of a new shape of toy vehicle might adequately describe the features for which protection is sought as being the features of shape and configuration of the vehicle as a whole. Similarly, the manufacturer of a tea or coffee pot of conventional shape upon which a new design has been applied may well describe the design registration as extending to the features of pattern or ornament applied to the article as shown in the accompanying drawings. The shape of the tea or coffee pot cannot be protected if it is conventional, but the new pattern can be.

The application procedure

The application procedure for registering a design is fairly straightforward and inexpensive. Photographs of the article are accepted but drawings are preferred and are usually prepared by specialist draughtsmen who are used to preparing drawings for patent and design applications. The drawings (or photographs) must provide comprehensive views of the article in question and, if it is three-dimensional, this usually means a front and rear view, side views, a top view and a perspective view. Where the article in question is essentially two-dimensional, such as with wallpaper, only a front view is required.

Search

As with patents and trade marks, the application is examined to see that the correct formalities have been met and a search is then carried out to determine if other similar designs have already been registered, or are in the process of being registered. It should, however, be noted that the search itself is not considered comprehensive by international standards and it can and often does happen that closely similar or even identical designs are registered for the same type of article. Because of this, the mere registration of a design should not necessarily be considered as proving its validity, and for important designs consideration may need to be given to carrying out private searches of the prior art designs to make doubly sure that none exist which are closely similar.

Registration

Once an application has been accepted the applicant receives a certificate of the type shown in Appendix 5 upon which are the applicant's details including the date of application, the statement of the article to which the design pertains and the claimed type of design covered, usually shape and configuration or pattern ornament. To this certificate is attached a set of the original drawings or photographs of the design and over which the monopoly for exclusive use extends.

Perhaps strangely, the design itself is not published in the same manner as is a patent or a registered trade mark, although the fact that a design registration has been granted to the applicant and a brief description of it is published by the official journal issued by the Patent Office every week. Accordingly, the only way in which members of the public can obtain full details of a registered design is by carrying out a search of the official records kept at the Designs Registry. To help in such a search designs are classified into various categories depending upon the type of article to which they pertain. The practical effect of this is that if a manufacturer designs a new product the only way in which he can be sure that manufacture, use or sale of the product would not infringe someone else's registered design is to have such a search carried out, as described in more detail in Chapter 9. Failure to carry out such clearance searches, which cost little compared to the negative consequences of a lawsuit for registered design infringement, can itself be prejudicial in that the Court expects manufacturers of new products to carry out reasonable enquiries beforehand to ensure that new products do not infringe the right of others. The same applies in respect of patents and trademarks.

As mentioned previously, the right given by registration of a design is not to exploit the design itself, but to exclude others from doing so. Even so, in practical terms registration of a design generally indicates that the owner of the design is free to exploit, but subject to the rights of owners of previous designs which may be similar and for which registration may already have been obtained.

Time and cost

It will be recalled from Chapter 2 that obtaining a patent is a slow and often painstaking process lasting up to four-and-a-half-years. Chapter 3 reveals that registration of a trade mark even in straightforward cases often takes two years to complete. Happily, registration of designs is much less complex and, perhaps because of this, can usually be completed within six to nine months. In relative terms the cost is very little and providing no unforeseen complications arise registration can be achieved for under £500 inclusive of professional adviser's fees and official government fees.

Conclusion

Design registration therefore constitutes a quick and inexpensive method of establishing an intellectual property right and these two factors should make such registration particularly attractive to manufacturers who make and sell products which rely to a significant extent on their external appearance. Curiously though, design registration has often been considered to be a 'poor man's patent' and may not be utilized to the fullest extent possible by manufacturers who, perhaps wrongly, believe that it is much better to spend more money and wait longer in order to get a patent for a new product. Each kind of intellectual property right is really quite distinct and, in the author's opinion, there can be very few newly designed products which would not benefit from design registration if eligible, whether or not the new product also incorporates some inventive concept which may be patentable. This is particularly so in respect of designs for products which do not have a very long shelf life in terms of fashionability, such as toys and domestic appliances. The advantage of obtaining protection for designs quickly and cheaply should not be overlooked, particularly if export markets are also of interest, where corresponding design registration can usually be obtained quite easily.

5 Copyright and the new design right

Changes to the law

Copyright law has changed significantly over the last 30 or so years as it has tried to keep abreast of new technologies and marketing philosophies. The most significant changes have occurred recently as a result of the enactment of the Copyright, Designs and Patents Act 1988 which completely recast the scope of copyright and fine-tuned the law to a degree which, it is to be hoped, will provide a legal framework for this subject well into the next century. A completely new concept has been introduced, called the 'design right', which may be considered as an independent form of intellectual property, but because it takes over part of what used to be covered by copyright law, is included in this chapter.

The modern law on copyright is so complex and covers so many subjects that this chapter describes only those aspects which are likely to be encountered by businessmen.

The problem with making changes in any kind of legislation is that at each such change a duality of approach is needed, defining what was the old law and defining what is the new law. If the law change introduces, say, criminal liability for what used to be a non-criminal offence there is no particular problem in applying the law change, since if the act complained of occurred before the change in the law then it is not a criminal act, whereas after the new law comes into effect it is criminal, and so on. Severe problems, however, occur when rights extending over many years are created by law, and those rights are then altered by subsequent changes in the law, or by changes which create new rights which did not exist before.

In respect of literary, dramatic, musical and artistic works, copyright generally lasts for 50 years after the end of the calendar year in which the author dies, whereas for sound recordings, films, broadcasts and cable programmes, the period is 50 years from the making of the work. Therefore, it will readily be seen that even less recent changes will have effect well into the next century, and depending upon when a copyright work was first created, different legal considerations will apply. Happily, as regards enforceability of copyright this state of affairs will not be taken over into the next century since Parliament has, by the latest Act, decreed a cutoff date of 1st August 1989 after which all copyright material is treated equally in terms of remedies available for infringement.

The 1956 Act

To illustrate the effects of the foregoing, it is useful to look back to the position which prevailed in the United Kingdom after the enactment of the Copyright Act 1956. Under that Act, copyright was defined as being a property right which arose automatically (there being no registration process) upon the creation of any original literary, dramatic, musical or artistic work. What was considered as a literary work generally meant books, plays, songs and other forms of written expression. Dramatic and musical works were self-explanatory and artistic works included drawings, paintings and photographs. To qualify for copyright protection, all that was needed was for each of these kinds of works to be created and then made public, which was an essential prerequisite for any copying by a third party. At that time there were no such things as word processors, computer programs, cassette tapes, compact discs, satellite broadcasts, photocopying machines, facsimile transmission machines and so on. Clearly, changes in legislation, or at least in the way existing legislation was to be interpreted, were required to keep pace with new technologies.

Amendment Act 1968

During the 1960s there was increasing concern over the apparent lack of protection for artistic drawings which were used as a basis for manufacturing artistic products which had not been the subject of design registration. This particularly applied to the jewellery trade, where it is still common practice for an item of jewellery to be drawn in full scale and for the drawing to be used by the craftsman to produce the finished piece, which is then sold to the public. The drawing itself is not normally published and, even if it were, it would be unlikely to be copied since it is not the drawing which is valuable to the owner, but the jewellery piece made from it. The 1956 Act excluded copyright for drawings and in the absence of a registered design there was no other protection.

As a consequence, there followed an amendment to the 1956 Act in the form of the Copyright (Designs) Amendment Act 1968 which extended copyright protection to drawings used to create published (i.e. made public usually by sale) works, such as actual items of jewellery for a term of 15 years, then the maximum duration of a registered design. By this mechanism, copying an item of jewellery thus became actionable in law, not because copyright was vested in the jewellery itself but because copyright was vested in the drawings and, even though they had not been seen by the copier in each case, nevertheless the copier had reproduced a three-dimensional representation of the two-dimensional drawings.

At first sight, this law change appeared a neat way of solving the underlying problem but its introduction had far-reaching effects which eventually resulted in the design right, featured in the 1988 Act. A problem arose because at the time of the 1968 Act it had already been held in law that engineering drawings, having been made with skill and labour, qualified as artistic works in their own right and therefore copying of such drawings, if they had been published, constituted copyright infringement. This must be reasonable, even if only for the fact that most engineering drawings also include features of design which are artistic in their nature.

A loophole in the law

For several years the 1968 Act was only seen as helping out those industries such as the jewellery trade until, in particular, the car manufacturers took an interest and concluded, quite rightly, that the law could be used to prevent unauthorized manufacture of spare parts for vehicles. The purchaser of a car usually has to replace parts such as the exhaust system at various intervals. When replacing the exhaust system there are two choices, the first and usually most expensive one being to buy a replacement exhaust system manufactured by or for the original manufacturer. The second choice is to purchase a similar exhaust system at lower cost made by a manufacturer specializing in replacement parts. The spare parts manufacturer does not need to copy the original exhaust system at all. In most cases the manufacturer does not, and simply produces an exhaust pipe which fits underneath the car and follows the same route as the original exhaust system. The forward end bolts onto the engine manifold, attachment clips are provided at the same points underneath the length of the vehicle body and the end of the exhaust system protrudes from underneath the vehicle at precisely the same point as the original.

Obviously, when each make of exhaust system is compared side-by-side they look almost identical, even though the replacement parts manufacturer has not and does not need to copy the original equipment manufacturer's design but inevitably he must reproduce the design if it is to fit the vehicle. No other design works. But the law provided that three-dimensional reproduction of a two-dimensional drawing infringed the copyright in the drawing, even an engineering drawing.

Lawsuits that changed the law again

Having spotted this loophole in the law, the original equipment manufacturers were, naturally enough, anxious to exploit the position and preserve for themselves the after-market sales for replacement parts. A series of lawsuits followed. Despite admirable and inventive defences being raised for several years the Courts consistently applied the law and held that where the replacement parts were closely similar to the original part then copyright infringement was established whether or not the replacement part manufacturer had deliberately copied the design of the original manufacture.

The most celebrated of these cases was *British Leyland* v. *Armstrong* where, fortunately, the defendant appealed all the way up to the House of Lords. In deciding the issue, their lordships recognized a quandary in that the copyright law had evolved to an extent which had all the hallmarks of patent protection, except that the subject matter did not need to be inventive, and that the protection afforded by copyright lasted much longer than for a patent. The further difficulty was that in previously applying the law in favour of the original equipment manufacturers, the effect was that owners of vehicles were being held to ransom by being able to purchase spare parts from only one source or from licensed manufacturers. Either way, the price was higher and the premium was paid to the copyright holder.

The problem was resolved in a remarkably fair and neat manner by their lordships deciding that in circumstances where the exercise of a copyright would effectively derogate from the rights of a purchaser to have a product repaired or serviced, such as the replacement of an old exhaust system by a new one, the purchaser has the right to choose whether or not to have such repair or service carried out by the original manufacturer, or by any other source. In those circumstances, whilst copyright may still exist it cannot be exercised against, particularly, manufacturers of spare parts.

The 1988 Act

Whilst the decision itself was well reasoned and commendable, nevertheless the anomaly of the copyright law recognizing the existence of a copyright which could not be exercised against a copier in some circumstances made it obvious that amendments to the law had to be introduced. When the law was changed the opportunity was also taken to introduce other amendments, as can be seen from the title of the 1988 Act, which reads:

> an Act to restate the law of copyright, with amendments; to make fresh provision as to the rights of performers and others in performances; to confer a design right

in original designs; to amend the Registered Designs Act 1949; to make provision with respect to patent agents and trade mark agents; to confer patents and designs jurisdiction on certain county courts; to amend the law of patents; to make provision with respect to devices designed to circumvent copy-protection of works in electronic form; to make fresh provision penalizing the fraudulent reception of transmissions; to make the fraudulent application or use of a trade mark an offence; to make provision for the benefit of the Hospital for Sick Children, Great Ormond Street London; to enable financial assistance to be given to certain international bodies; and for connected purposes.

As an aside, the reader may be interested in the reference to the Great Ormond Street Hospital. The new Act grants copyright in perpetuity to the hospital in the J. M. Barrie novel *Peter Pan,* a highly laudable but perhaps questionable departure from the basic and internationally recognized principle that a copyright cannot last forever.

Under the new Act, copyright now subsists in original, dramatic, musical or artistic works (as with the 1956 Act), sound recordings, films, broadcasts or cable programmes, and typographical arrangements of published editions as follows:

- An artistic work means a graphic work, photograph, sculpture or collage, irrespective of artistic quality, a work of architecture being a building or a model for a building, or a work of artistic craftsmanship.
- A literary work means any work other than a dramatic or musical work which is written, spoken or sung, and includes a table or compilation and, specifically, a computer programme.
- A dramatic work includes a work of dance or mime, but this is not an exhaustive definition.
- Finally, a musical work means a work consisting of music, exclusive of any words or action intended to be sung, spoken or performed with the music.

It will be seen from the foregoing that we now have a fully codified definition as to what constitutes a copyright work under the new Act which extends well beyond the definitions to be found in the 1956 Act, as amended by the 1968 Act. Many of the changes are designed simply to clarify and confirm broad interpretations which have been given previously by the Courts before the new Act became law. Particularly useful is the confirmation that copyright work extends to computer programs, which have become increasingly important as changes in modern society increasingly rely upon the use of computers.

'Conversion damages'

A significant change brought about by the new law is not the definition of what constitutes a copyright work, but the removal of what was often considered to be a particularly unfair penalty for direct copying where the damages obtainable by a plaintiff could in most instances amount to the monetary value of all of the products which had been produced as a result of the copying, the so-called 'conversion damages'. Before the new Act, a successful copyright claim was often associated with enormous monetary loss for the defendant, which was grossly unfair when compared to the more usual level of damages awarded for infringement of other forms of intellectual property, based upon actual damages suffered by the plaintiff or an account of profits earned by the defendant.

The design right

Even so, without doubt the most significant change brought about by the new Act is the introduction of what is called the design right, which is intended to replace that portion of the old copyright law which had been developed to meet the needs of jewellery manufacturers and the like but which ended up providing, for a few years, an artificial monopoly for car manufacturers on spare parts. This is not to say that the new design right restores car manufacturers to the position they enjoyed before the House of Lords intervened, since the new law avoids having to deal with the derogation of a purchaser's rights to have a product manufactured and serviced wherever he chooses, by making exclusions which effectively do the same job.

Exclusions from copyright protection

Now excluded from copyright protection is the design of any aspect of the shape or configuration (whether internal or external) of the whole or part of an article. Instead, this is now the subject matter of the newly created design right which, as with copyright, arises automatically upon the creation of an original design by a qualified individual or person, i.e. citizens or companies which are habitually resident or established in the United Kingdom or other countries of the EEC, together with corresponding persons or companies established in other jurisdictions where the qualification has been extended by Order in Council. Excluded from protection under the new design right are methods or principles of construction and surface decoration. Most importantly, there are excluded features of shape or configuration which:

1. enable the article to be connected to or placed in, around or against, another article so that either article may perform its function, or
2. are dependent upon the appearance of another article of which the article is intended by the designer to form an integral part.

These latter two exclusions are conveniently referred to as the 'must fit' and 'must match' exclusions. The way in which each operates can be conveniently illustrated again with reference to the car industry. A vehicle silencer is covered by the first exclusion and therefore does not qualify for design right protection, and the vehicle body panel is covered by the second exclusion, even though the panel may be extremely ornate in design terms.

Ownership of a design right

Ownership of a design right is decided in precisely the same way as for copyright (and for that matter the right to obtain patents and registered designs) in that the designer owns the right, unless it is created in pursuance of a paid commission or in the course of employment. If the design is created in pursuance of a paid commission the person commissioning the design is the owner and, similarly, where an employee is employed to create a design then upon creation of the design it is owned by the employer. There is an exception to this general principle where the design is created in other than a qualifying country and is first marketed in the United Kingdom or a qualifying country by a person, company or firm which is exclusively authorized or licensed to do so. It is not clear how these exceptions will operate in practice and it is possible that difficulties may arise in defining what is meant by 'exclusively authorized' or 'exclusively licensed' when, without the design right being already created, the concept of granting exclusive rights is necessarily meaningless.

Duration of a design right

It was seen earlier that the duration of a copyright varies according to the type of copyright work and the circumstances in which the work was first published. Similarly, the duration of a design right is variable and expires:

1. 15 years from the end of the calendar year in which the design was first recorded in a design document, or an article was first made to the design, whichever occurs first, or
2. if articles made to the design are made available for sale or hire anywhere in the world within 5 years from the end of that calendar year, 10 years from the end of the calendar year in which that sale or hire first occurred.

It is to be expected that disputes will arise as to when a design right should expire and it is perhaps a pity that Parliament did not suggest and provide a more positive scheme, i.e. through registration, to provide more certainty and less room for argument, even if such a scheme were only voluntary but had the effect of constituting a prima facie ownership of the existence of the design right in any subsequent litigation for infringement. Alternatively, owners of a design right could be required to indicate on published documents or finished articles the year of first publication or manufacture so as to make calculation of the proper term relatively straightforward, bearing in mind that those interested in utilizing designs of the type covered by the new design right are likely to be involved in the manufacturing industries and require certainty of return for investment made.

Conclusion

This chapter has discussed in very brief and general terms the major features of the existing law of copyright and the new design right. It will be apparent that the changes bought about by this new legislation are likely to affect more than ever the way in which business is conducted and how it is planned. It is no longer enough to regard, in particular, copyright as being some mystical form of protection available for artistically gifted people. A sobering thought is that almost every letter, advertisement, company report, design drawing, speech or new product made creates a new copyright or design right, or infringes someone else's!

6 Confidential information or know-how

This is the fifth general category of intellectual property right and is distinguished from the other four in not being recognized by the existence of any statutory legislation, although this does not mean that know-how cannot be legally protected. Protection comes from the common law in a variety of ways, including the laws on breach of contract, breach of fiduciary duty and related causes of action.

What is know-how?

Know-how arises as a result of experience gained in, typically, making products or operating processes. The confidential information obtained from such experience is not in itself protectable by means of a patent, copyright or registered design but, nevertheless, as long as it remains secret the information gives the owner an edge over the competition, or at least an edge over new entrants into the same kind of business. To illustrate, a glass manufacturer may learn through experience when designing a new glass production facility in an overseas territory, that for a given potential market for the glass the manufacturing facility should ideally be of a particular size in order to optimize production within the constraints of a given budget dictated by the likely market share for the product. Having established the optimum size of the glass-making facility, the know-how gained through experience may also suggest the most suitable types of materials for construction of the refractory lining for the glass furnace, whether the furnace should be powered by electricity or gas, if gas then what type to use to achieve the most economical returns, the layout of the gas burners within the furnace to achieve optimum uniformity of temperature spread and so on. Each individual item of knowledge collectively adds a little to the value of the entire know-how and it will be apparent that savings in construction and running costs of just a few per cent, or producing just a few per cent more glass than would otherwise be possible, can make the know-how extremely valuable in commercial terms.

Know-how is not limited to process industries such as glass-making. It can extend to almost any business including the fast food industry where knowledge of a recipe for a particular food item may provide consistent results which help to sell the product or make it more attractive. Knowing what are the best ingredients for the menu offered by a fast food outlet and where they can be purchased, the optimum storage times for the raw materials, the most economic quantities which should be purchased for a given market share and so on all amount to valuable know-how which can improve profitability or maintain market share of the business, or both.

Keeping know-how secret

Know-how remains valuable only if it is kept secret. Public disclosure puts the know-how in the public domain and nothing can be done to stop third parties from utilizing it for their own benefit. Accordingly, if know-how is to be preserved as a proprietary asset of a company steps have to be taken to ensure that the information does not leak away through carelessness, or lack of control over the activities of employees or persons to whom the know-how has been licensed. This usually means ensuring restricted access to the workplace if the proprietary know-how can easily be learned by a third party simply visiting the site. Perhaps more importantly, it also means imposing contractual conditions on directors and employees of a company, subcontractors who work for the company, and licensees who have obtained access to the information in return for payment of a royalty fee.

Directors

In most instances, directors of companies are considered by the Courts to owe a fiduciary duty to the company to keep its affairs confidential and to promote the interests of the company to the exclusion of all else. This duty survives any termination of the appointment as a director so that, generally speaking, unauthorized disclosure of know-how by an ex-director of the company is actionable.

Employees

The same is not always true in connection with employees of a company, who are permitted more latitude in the nature of the obligations they owe to the company during and after employment with the company. This does not mean that an employee can simply make use of a company's proprietary know-how once employment has been terminated, but it does mean that experience gained by the employee during his employment is free for that employee to take once the employment has terminated.

An example of this principle was the case of *Faccenda Chicken* v. *Fowler*, in that case a most appropriately named defendant. The plaintiff was in the business of selling chickens and related products with the aid of a fleet of vans, each van driver being assigned a particular sales area, the object being to visit customers on a regular basis to sell the products direct, rather than through the intermediary of a retail store. Mr Fowler was employed in this capacity and in due course decided to set up business for himself in the same area. Naturally enough, he knew the identities of the customers of Faccenda Chicken, their preferences as to the type of product required and, significantly, the prices charged by Faccenda Chicken. He was also, of course, well-known to the customers and was therefore able quickly to establish himself in the same line of business. The Court held in those circumstances that without there being any express contractual provisions preventing Mr Fowler from setting up a rival business and utilizing knowledge gained whilst employed with Faccenda Chicken, he was free to do as he pleased.

This case illustrates the benefit of utilizing comprehensive employment contracts, particularly for those businesses which would otherwise be vulnerable in the event that an employee decided to set up or work for a rival business. However, it is important to note that if it is to be enforced an employment contract must be fair and reasonable in the circumstances of any particular case. Employment and other contracts of this nature can and will be found invalid by the Courts, either partially or wholly, if they contain clauses which are clearly unfair to the employee, such as those which constitute an unfair restraint of trade once the employment has terminated.

Subcontractors

Subcontractors may also properly be the subject of contractual conditions governing their employment, whether they are subcontracted to carry out work for the business itself, such as internal repair and maintenance work, or if they carry out work on behalf of the business. In each case, similar considerations apply and it is not difficult, or expensive, to have a solicitor draw up a standard short-form agreement in which the subcontractor is obligated to keep the affairs of the company secret and not to disclose any information obtained to third parties without the prior written approval of the company.

Licences to third parties

More problematical is the situation where know-how is licensed to a third party. The third party may be an unrelated arm's-length company interested in entering a particular line of business, or could even be a company set up as a joint venture with a third-party partner in which the know-how is licensed to the joint venture company. In many instances, licensing of this type occurs overseas and is fraught with difficulties and dangers which can usually only be minimized by very careful planning and a carefully worded contract. Above all, the licensee or joint venture partner, as the case may be, must be trusted, otherwise there are simply too many ways in which the licenser can end up losing rights in proprietary know-how. Even if a carefully worded contract has been entered into which provides remedies for breach, this is not the end of the story since in many jurisdictions bureaucratic or legal obstacles can arise which effectively prevent the enforcement of terms in a contract, or the enforcement overseas of a judgement obtained in a UK Court. Difficulties of this nature are described in more detail in Chapter 8 but are mentioned briefly here in order to illustrate the vulnerability of know-how as a type of intellectual property, as compared to the four other general categories which usually survive after any dispute whether or not there has been any breach of contract.

Know-how possessed by several companies

A final aspect about know-how which is worth mentioning but may not be immediately apparent is that know-how need not necessarily be unique to any particular party. Several companies may each possess similar know-how and each cannot stop the others from utilizing their own know-how if it has been fairly obtained through experience. Even so, if one company obtains know-how from another improperly, such as by inducing breach of contract on the part of an employee, or even by engaging in industrial espionage, the Court will usually, if asked to do so, grant a permanent injunction against the company to prevent utilization of the know-how until it fairly enters the public domain.

7 Infringement of intellectual property rights

Most people know when their rights as individuals are being infringed, sometimes by people trespassing on their property, sometimes by tenants being harassed by unscrupulous landlords, and sometimes even by an invasion of privacy brought about by the publication of a secretly taken photograph. The same is generally also true for infringement of intellectual property rights and owners of such rights generally know if they should or should not feel aggrieved by the actions of a third party. What is not generally known is the extent to which third parties can encroach upon the rights of intellectual property owners without fear of adverse consequences and, equally, how far intellectual property rights sometimes extend beyond what may be considered an obvious and fair reach. This chapter explores what is meant by infringement and the next chapter will explain the legal remedies available.

We have seen from Chapters 2 to 6 that intellectual property rights come in many different forms, some having to be pursued and obtained at relatively great cost in terms of time and money, as in the case of patents, registered trade marks and registered designs, but others arising automatically as in the case of copyrights and common law rights in trade marks. Finally, we have know-how which is obtained through experience and retained through secrecy. It is therefore obvious that there can be no general definition of what is meant by infringement of all of these rights, other than perhaps the general statement that an infringement constitutes unfair dealing or exploitation of such rights without the consent of the owner.

In this chapter we look at the statutory and common law definitions of what constitutes infringement, some of which may come as a surprise to the reader.

Patents

The grant of a patent gives the owner (which may be an individual or a company) the right to exclude others from making use of the patented invention for as long as the patent remains in force in the United Kingdom. The claims define the scope of the invention and, clearly, anyone making an article or utilizing a process as defined by the claims of the patent infringes the patent. However, additional acts not immediately covered by the patent claims can also constitute infringement and, conversely, acts which appear to be covered by the patent claims may not, depending upon the particular circumstances.

Definition of infringement

A person infringes a patent, subject to the exceptions listed later, in the following circumstances:

1. Where the invention is a product he makes, disposes of, offers to dispose of, uses or imports it into the United Kingdom or keeps it in the United Kingdom whether for disposal or otherwise. Obviously, this is a very wide definition and appears to cover any dealing in a product which is covered by a patent.
2. If the invention is a process, he uses it or offers it for use in the United Kingdom when he knows, or it is obvious to a reasonable person in the circumstances, that its use without the consent of the proprietor would be an infringement of the patent. Note here the difference from the first definition in that knowledge or reasonable knowledge that the process is patented is required in order to infringe.
3. If the invention is a process, he disposes of, offers to dispose of, uses or imports any product obtained directly by means of that process or keeps any such products whether for disposal or otherwise. Note here that a patent for a process is infringed by importation of a product manufactured outside of the United Kingdom but made in accordance with the process, even though the process may not have been patented in the country of origin of the product.
4. Where a person supplies or offers to supply in the United Kingdom a person other than a licensee or other person entitled to work the invention with any of the means relating to an essential element of the invention, for putting the invention into effect when he knows, or it is obvious to a reasonable person in the circumstances, that those means are suitable for putting, and are intended to put, the invention into effect in the United Kingdom. This kind of infringement is often termed 'contributory infringement' and requires a knowledge that the supply of component parts or materials for manufacturing the patented apparatus or carrying out the patented process will in fact be used by an unauthorized party to do just that.

It will be seen from this list that the definitions of infringement are perhaps surprisingly wide and leave room for argument as to whether, for example, a person knew or ought to have known that an article imported into the United Kingdom had been made in accordance with a patented process.

Exceptions

There are, however, exceptions to the above list of infringements and a person does not infringe a patent in the following circumstances.

1. The contributory infringement referred to in (4) above does not apply in respect of the supply or offer of staple commercial products, unless the supply or offer is made for the purpose of inducing the person supplied or, as the case may be, the person to whom the offer is made, to infringe a patent relating to a product. Note in particular that this exception does not relate to the supply of staple commercial products to persons infringing a patent for a process. For example, if the patent concerns a process for making glass then the mere supply of sand by a third party to an infringer of that process would not constitute an infringement of the patent, unless the purpose was to induce infringement.
2. When acts are done privately and not for commercial purposes.
3. When acts are done for experimental purposes relating to the subject matter of the invention, for example by competitors when trying to determine the efficacy of a patented chemical compound such as a pharmaceutical drug.
4. The preparation in a pharmacy of a medicine for an individual in accordance with a prescription given by a registered medical or dental practitioner, or dealing with the medicine so prepared.
5. Temporary use of the invention exclusively for the needs of a relevant ship, within the body of the ship or in its machinery, tackle, apparatus or other accessories where the ship has temporarily or accidentally entered British territorial waters.
6. The use of a patented product or process in the body or operation of an aircraft, hovercraft or vehicle which has temporarily or accidentally entered or is crossing the United Kingdom, or the use of accessories for such an aircraft, hovercraft or vehicle.
7. The use of an exempted aircraft which has lawfully entered or is lawfully crossing the United Kingdom. The term 'exempted' here means certain aircraft which have been excluded from seizure in respect of patent claims by the Civil Aviation Act 1949.

The complexities of infringement

It will be apparent that simply looking at the claims of the patent is not enough to determine whether or not a person (including of course a company) infringes it. Complexities arise, in particular, in deciding whether or not a person is reasonable in assuming knowledge or lack of knowledge of a patented product or process, or that the supply of staple commercial materials are to be used by an unauthorized party to infringe a patent. It should also be noted that innocent infringement by a person who did not know of the existence of a patent is not exempted from the definitions of infringement given above, although, as will be discussed in the next chapter, in some instances innocent infringers may escape liability for their deeds.

Apart from acts of contributory infringement, direct infringement of a patent is established with reference to the actual words used in the claims and, as a general rule, to infringe a patent a person must utilize each and every feature of at least one patent claim. If a patent claim specifies, say, six essential features of the invention and an alleged infringer utilizes only five, then normally there is no infringement. There are two kinds of infringement, the first being textual and the second being what may be loosely described as 'substitution infringement'.

Textual infringement

Textual infringement, as the term suggests, means infringement in accordance with the actual text of one or more claims of the patent. If the text of a particular claim specifies that a product or process must have certain features and if the product or process complained of has those features then there is textual infringement, whether or not the product or process also possesses other features.

Substitution infringement

If the complained-of product or process does not possess all of the features in the claim then there cannot be textual infringement. Thus, the only thing left for a potential plaintiff to consider is whether there is infringement as a result of substitution of one or more of the features specified in the claim for equivalent features which have essentially the same effect. Included in this kind of infringement is the use of obvious mechanical equivalents for features contained in the claim, such as the substitution of a spring for a rubber band. Even so, what matters in considering infringement of a claim by way of substitution of one feature for another is the purpose of the claim, as taught by the patent specification.

In one case, a defendant tried to 'design around' a patent for a new and useful kind of door lintel constructed from folded steel plate and in which the claimed invention specified that the rear plate used in the lintel was disposed 'vertically' with respect to the lower portion of the lintel. The defendants assumed, quite wrongly, that by offsetting the rear plate by 6 degrees from the vertical, they would escape infringement of the claim but the Court held that the purpose of the claim was not to mean, with reference to the word 'vertical', precisely vertical but a rear plate which was approximately vertical. Possibly offsetting the plate by 10 or 15 degrees may have avoided infringement but, in mechanical terms, it would have made the lintel much weaker and therefore unusable.

In taking a pragmatic view of that the Court reinforced an old established principle that the owner of an invention should not be deprived of the fruits of his labour by others trying to draw clever distinctions between the intended scope of an invention and the words actually used to describe it in the claims.

The other side of the coin is a patent claim which limits itself by a choice of words which clearly differentiate the features claimed from similar features which may be used in substitution. A particular example of this arose in the case of a depilatory device which utilized the principle that when a helically wound spring is bent about its longitudinal access and then rotated, the outermost portion between each successive winding of the spring opens up rather like a jaw, whereas the corresponding inner portion becomes clamped tightly shut. Upon rotation of the spring over an area of skin from which protrudes hair, the hair tends to be drawn into the closed end of each jaw and is then pulled out.

The patent claim specified that a 'helically wound spring' must be used. Whilst clearly quite a painful process the depilatory device nevertheless sold very well and, perhaps naturally enough, attracted the attention of competitors. One such competitor produced a device which worked in a similar manner but did not use a helically wound spring for pulling out the hair. Instead, it utilized a rod of circular cross-section made of rubber-like material and into which were cut a series of parallel slots so that the entire rod resembled a set of individual discs joined together near to the central hub of each disc. Bending and rotating the rod produced the same result. Thus, a competing depilatory device was put onto the market which sold very well and did not fall within the scope of the claims of the patent. The question, of course, was whether or not it was obvious to substitute a helically wound spring for a rubber rod cut in the shape of a series of adjacent discs. The Court found that it was not and hence the patent was not infringed.

Conclusion

It will be apparent that infringement of a patent is not easily established with any certainty and the opinion of a patent agent, even in cases where there does not appear to be any doubt, will provide a sound basis for deciding what to do, or even if there is anything that can be done.

Registered trade marks

The statutory definition of what constitutes infringement of a registered trade mark is not nearly so complex as that relating to the infringement of a patent, but this does not make the task of deciding what constitutes infringement an easy one, in view of the very different characteristics of the rights granted by registration of a trade mark. Infringement of a patent is established with reference to the patent claims, an infringer either does or does not utilize the features listed in the claims of the patent, or utilizes obviously equivalent features in substitution for one or more of those listed. However, registration of a trade mark, whilst protecting the same mark from being copied, also provides protection against the use by others of confusingly similar trade marks in respect of the goods or services for which the trade mark is registered. From this simple concept stems the realization that the boundaries of what constitutes infringement cannot be precisely defined and depend upon whether the Court, when comparing the registered trade mark with the alleged infringing mark, feels that they are or are not confusingly similar. Obviously, if the infringer's mark is identical to the registered trade mark then the issue is clear cut, and equally if the infringing mark is only slightly different then, as a general rule, this will not provide an escape route from liability for the infringer.

Definitions of infringement

A person infringes a registered trade mark in the following circumstances.

1. If the trade mark is registered in respect of goods, that person uses without any authorization in the course of trade a mark identical with or nearly resembling the registered trade mark in respect of any of the goods for which the mark is registered, so that the mark is likely to be taken as either a trade mark, in the normally accepted sense; or by using the mark on or in relation to the goods, including advertising circulars or other advertisements issued to the public, so as to import a reference to the trade mark owner or a licensee of the trade mark owner.
2. In the case of a trade mark registered in respect of services, if the person uses an identical or nearly resembling mark in respect of some or all of the services for which the trade mark is registered, again so that the use of the mark is likely to be taken as use as a trade mark; or in a case in which the use is at or near the place where the services are available or performed, or the use is in an advertisement issued to the public, as importing a reference to the trade mark owner or a licensee.

3. The final definition of infringement relates to breaches of contract between the trade mark owner or licensee and the ultimate purchaser of the goods. Where obligations are entered into on the part of the purchaser (including any subsequent owner having knowledge of the contractual obligations) and the purchaser carries out or authorizes any act which is in breach of the contractual obligations, then in these circumstances the following acts are considered also to constitute infringement:
   (a) the application of the trade mark upon the goods after they have been altered in any manner specified in the contract regarding their state or condition, style or packing;
   (b) when the trade mark appears on the goods, the alteration, part removal or part obliteration of it;
   (c) when the trade mark appears on the goods, and there is also other matter present indicating a connection in the course of trade between the proprietor or registered user of the mark and the goods, the removal or obliteration, whether wholly or partly, of the trade mark unless all the other matter is removed or obliterated;
   (d) when the trade mark appears on the goods, placing any other trade mark on them; and
   (e) when the trade mark appears on the goods, the addition to them of any other matter in writing that is likely to injure the reputation of the trade mark.

It will therefore be seen that where goods are sold on condition that, for instance, the trade mark should not be obliterated, or that no other trade mark should be applied to them afterwards, non-compliance on the part of the purchaser can constitute an infringement of the registered trade mark. However, as will be seen from Chapter 15, European Community law is unlikely to recognize the validity of such infringement rights if they run contrary to Community law, in particular if they impose upon a purchaser restrictions which are unfair or which run contrary to the general principles of 'exhaustion of rights' and free trade.

Thus, there are essentially three forms of infringement, one being direct infringement by selling goods or offering services with the use of the same mark, or one which nearly resembles the registered trade mark, in the course of trade. The second is 'importing a reference' to the registered trade mark, whether or not the infringer is selling goods or offering services under or by reference to an altogether different trade mark. And the third arises when a purchaser breaches express obligations governing use of the mark after a product has been purchased. However, this third type of infringement is quite rare since most goods are not purchased under any specific contract concerning the trade mark but, rather, under normal sale and purchase conditions. This means that for most purposes only the first and second types of infringement need be considered.

Direct infringement

Direct infringement can arise innocently through an incautious choice of a mark which is subsequently found to be too similar to a registered trade mark covering the same goods or services. Deliberate use of a mark the same as or similar to one which is already registered is usually prompted by a desire to take unfair advantage of the reputation and goodwill associated with the registered mark. Whatever the motive, the infringement is dealt with in the same manner by the Courts, as discussed in the next chapter.

Importing a reference

Infringement by importing a reference to a registered trade mark means that almost any use of a registered trade mark by a competitor such as, for example, in the form of comparative advertising, is likely to infringe even if this use makes it clear that the registered trade mark is being used only for comparison purposes so that the trade or public are not actually confused or deceived into thinking that both trade marks are owned by the same proprietor.

In some industries it appears that comparative advertising has become an accepted practice but this does not alter the fact that the trade mark owner in each case does have a right of action, and caution should therefore be exercised when considering using a trade mark owned by someone else for any purposes in the course of trade, including comparative advertising.

Close resemblance

It will be noted from the above that a trade mark is also infringed by the use of another mark which 'nearly resembles' the registered trade mark and from this it will be apparent that there is always room for argument and uncertainty as to whether or not a court will agree that the defendant's mark nearly resembles that of the plaintiff. In practice, what is meant by this phrase are marks which are confusingly or deceptively similar but, again, certainty of infringement can only be established after a trial.

Exceptions

As with patents, there are also exceptions to what constitutes infringement of registered trade marks. These statutory exceptions can be summarized as follows.

1. If the use by another person of the registered trade mark is not in the course of trade then it does not constitute infringement of the trade mark. Thus, the mere reference to a registered trade mark in a book, this book for example, does not constitute an act of infringement provided, of course, the book is not sold under or by reference to the registered trade mark.
2. A trade mark is not infringed by a person if it is used in relation to goods connected in the course of trade with the proprietor or a licensee of the registered trade mark if, as to those goods or a bulk of which they form part, the proprietor or licensee has applied the trade mark and has not subsequently removed or obliterated it, or has at any time expressly or impliedly consented to the use of the trade mark.

   This must be so since, otherwise, it would be impossible to sell a second-hand car by reference to the make and model without infringing the registered trade mark of the car manufacturer. Reference to 'a bulk of which they form part' is generally held to mean that it is permissible to refer to a registered trade mark when selling a product comprised primarily of goods upon which the trade mark has been applied such as, for example, referring to a garment as having been made from a particular fabric which is itself sold under or by reference to a registered trade mark, e.g. LYCRA. However, this does not mean that the manufacturer of the garment can sell it as if it were a garment made by the trade mark owner since, clearly, it would not be and such use would constitute trade mark infringement and also certainly would constitute a passing off under the common law.
3. A person also escapes liability for infringement of a registered trade mark if he uses the mark in relation to goods adapted to form part of, or to be accessory to, other goods in relation to which the registered trade mark has been used, if the use of the mark is reasonably necessary in order to indicate that the goods are so adapted to form part of or be accessory to the other goods, and neither the purpose nor the effect of the use of the trade mark is to indicate otherwise than a connection in the course of trade between any person and the goods.

   Thus, it is permissible for someone to sell parts or accessories of other goods made by someone else and to refer to the registered trade mark if reference to it is reasonably necessary for selling the part or accessory, but only if the trade or public do not thereby consider that there is some connection between the vendor and the registered trade mark owner or a licensee of the registered trade mark. In practice, this will usually mean that the part or accessory must also be referred to by reference to an entirely different trade mark or trade name in order clearly to distinguish the origin of the goods. The reference to the registered trade mark must not, of course, be such that purchasers are in any way confused as to the origin or quality of the goods.

4. With a registered service mark, the right given by registration is not infringed by the use of the mark by a person in relation to services to which the proprietor of the mark or a licensee has applied the mark, where the purpose and effect of the use of the mark is to indicate, if factually true, that those services have been performed by the proprietor or a licensee. Thus if, for example, a firm of chartered accountants were to register their name as a trade mark in respect of accountancy services, the firm could not prevent the use of their name by a company in a share prospectus to indicate that the firm are the accountants used by the company.
5. There is also no infringement of a trade mark registered for services if it is used by a person in relation to services the provision of which is connected in the course of business with the proprietor or a licensee of the mark, where the proprietor or registered user has at any time expressly or impliedly consented to the use of the mark. As with trade marks registered for goods, it is also not an infringement for a person to use the mark in relation to services available for use with other services, if the use of the registered trade mark is reasonably necessary in order to indicate that the services are available for such use and neither the purpose nor the effect of the use of the registered trade mark is to indicate otherwise.

   Hence, as with similar provisions in (3) above in respect of trade marks registered for particular goods, it is permissible to use a trade mark registered for services where the use is reasonably necessary, provided that it does not indicate that there is a connection with the trade mark owner when in fact there is not such a connection.
6. Finally, the use of a registered trade mark in respect of the goods or services for which it is registered cannot, in law, be an infringement of another mark registered for the same goods or services. Presumably, this is a consequence of other provisions in the law which state that it is not lawful to register a mark which is identical or confusingly similar to an already registered mark in respect of the same or similar goods or services. Even so, it can and does happen that mistakes are made and occasionally the use of a registered trade mark may cause deception or confusion of the trade or public in view of its similarity to another mark which is also registered. In those circumstances, the owner of the other registered mark may still have a cause of action,

but under the common law to prevent acts of passing off, discussed later in this chapter.

An additional exception

In addition to the above statutory definitions of what does not constitute infringement of a registered trade mark, there is one more avenue of escape for a potential or actual defendant, which concerns marks registered in Part B of the Register. It will be recalled from Chapter 3 that the Trade Marks Register is split into two parts, Part A being reserved for marks which are considered distinctive, either inherently so or by having acquired distinctiveness through use; and Part B being reserved for those marks which are only considered to be capable of distinguishing the goods of the trade mark owner from those of others. In practice there is no difference between the definition of what constitutes infringement of Part A and Part B marks. However, a defendant can escape liability for acts of infringement if he establishes to the satisfaction of the Court that the use of the trade mark is not likely to deceive or cause confusion, and will not be taken as indicating a connection in the course of trade between the goods or services on or with which the trade mark has been used and the owner of the registered trade mark or his licensee. Note here that the onus is firmly on the defendant to establish these facts to the satisfaction of the Court and thus it is hardly surprising that, to date, this theoretical escape from liability for acts of infringement of a Part B registered trade mark has never succeeded in the United Kingdom since it was first introduced in 1938.

Conclusion

From the above it will be seen that determining which acts constitute infringement can be highly complex and requires expert advice, even in what may appear to be the most straightforward of cases, and before any offensive or defensive action is taken.

Registered designs

It was seen from Chapter 4 that a design is registrable only in respect of a particular article or set of articles and it therefore follows that infringement of a registered design can only be by the use of the same or a similar design on the same type of article or set of articles. Registration of the design gives the owner in the United Kingdom, the Isle of Man and certain overseas territories such as Hong Kong the exclusive right to make or import for sale or for use for the purposes of any trade or business, or to sell, hire or offer for sale or hire, any article in respect of which the design is registered, being an article to which the registered design or a design not substantially different from it has been applied, and to make anything for enabling any such article to be made whether in the United Kingdom or elsewhere.

Definitions of infringement

Thus, a registered design is infringed by anyone who:

1. Without the authorization of the owner makes or imports for sale or for use for the purposes of any trade or business, or to sell, hire or offer for sale or hire, any article in respect of which the design is registered and on which the design has been applied, or a design which is not substantially different from the registered design has been applied.
2. Makes anything for enabling any such article to be made, even if the article is to be made outside of the United Kingdom or the Isle of Man.

It will once again be apparent that the definition of infringement of a registered design, other than where the exact design has been used on the same article for which the design is registered, depends upon whether or not a court feels that the alleged infringing design is 'not substantially different' from the registered design. Note here that the test is a reversal of the test for infringement of a registered trade mark, where an infringing mark must be either identical or must nearly resemble the registered trade mark. Even so, in practice the Courts have tended to hold the view that to infringe a registered design the infringer must either apply the same design to the same article or must apply a closely similar design to the same article. This does not mean, of course, that in order to escape infringement it is simply necessary for a person to make minor changes to a design since, clearly, the overall impression given by the design in each case will be the same.

Where the design of the article is fairly unusual, even the use of a design which may have been derived independently and does not copy any specific part but, nevertheless, still gives the same overall impression as that of the registered design, is also likely to infringe. In those circumstances, the owner of the registered design enjoys quite broad protection from copying by the use of designs utilizing the same general design concept. On the other hand, for products such as hair dryers, it is often the case that the design registered only differs relatively marginally from other designs already known and perhaps even already registered. In those circumstances, it is clear that a much narrower definition of what constitutes infringement must be applied so that only a hair dryer having the identical design or a design very similar would be found to infringe.

Exceptions

Exceptions to what constitutes infringement are almost non-existent, other than the right of any government department to use any registered design for the services of the Crown, either with or without the permission of the proprietor. Such a Crown user right is almost never exercised although, when it is, the proprietor is still normally entitled to a fair royalty which, if the parties cannot agree as to the terms, can be settled if necessary by the Court.

There is a defence in terms of liability to any party who innocently infringes a registered design. Damages are not awarded against any defendant who proves that at the date of the infringement he was not aware and had no reasonable ground for supposing that the design was registered. This does not mean that a defendant can simply allege or assert, whether truthfully or otherwise, that he did not know the design was registered in order to escape liability. The Court, in determining whether a defendant can hide behind a defence of innocence, will normally proceed on the assumption that it is reasonable for the manufacturer or vendor of a new design of product to carry out enquiries beforehand to determine whether the design has already been registered by a third party. Failure to carry out such enquiries will usually prove fatal to any such defence, even if the product is sold in complete ignorance of the rights of the proprietor of the design. Particular care must be taken in regard to products which are imported. If there is any possibility that the design of the article in question is registered in the United Kingdom, this should be checked beforehand, otherwise the importer and/or vendor will be liable and, usually, the manufacturer will not be unless the design is also registered in the country of manufacture.

Perhaps surprisingly, it will also be seen from the foregoing that infringement is also established by making it possible for someone else to make the article elsewhere, even in a country where the design has not even been registered. Clearly, it should not be right for one person to assist another in infringing a UK registered design by supplying, for example, a manufacturer of teapots with transfers depicting a design pattern to enable the manufacturer to apply the pattern to the teapots if the teapots then constitute an infringement of someone else's registered design. However, the words used in the statutory definition of this kind of infringement, often called 'contributory infringement', can be read much wider and could also include even the mere supply of staple commercial products by one party to another, who then proceeds to use the products to manufacture articles infringing a third-party design. Although the Courts have tended to restrict the scope of the statutory definition of contributory infringement so as to exclude such a possibility, the matter is by no means settled law. However, it is to be expected that all but the most blatant acts of assisting in the infringement of a registered design would be ignored by the Court.

Passing off

It was mentioned in Chapter 1 that passing off is a common law right of action and, accordingly, there is no statutory definition as to what constitutes this tort, or civil wrongdoing. However, over the many years that such a right of action has been available, the Courts have had plenty of time to consider a wide variety of issues raised by such cases and from which certain principles have been identified, which are now used by the Courts to establish whether or not a person is guilty of passing off his goods or services as or for the goods or services of another. Even so, it should be noted in particular that as a body of case law, passing off is not static and is constantly evolving to keep pace with changes in technology and marketing tactics.

To establish a case of passing off, there must first of all be a reputation and that reputation can be in a host of things, such as in a trade mark, trade name, company name, product packaging, type of decor used in a hotel or restaurant, slogans used in advertising and so on. Without a reputation being enjoyed by one party it is not possible for another party to trade off or exploit that reputation and thus pass off his goods or services as or for those of the other. In some instances, the reputation may have been earned over a period of several years but in others the reputation can be established in a relatively short period of time, particularly if accompanied by high volume sales or heavy advertising.

Definitions of passing off

In classic cases of passing off the following five integers will usually be present:

1. a misrepresentation,
2. made by a trader (which includes persons trading in goods or services), in the course of trade in goods or services,
3. to customers or prospective customers,
4. which is calculated to deceive or cause confusion (whether deliberately or innocently even though the term 'calculated' is used), and
5. which actually causes deception or confusion, or is likely to do so if the acts complained of are merely threatened or have just commenced.

It will therefore be seen that the law relating to passing off is primarily based upon the end result, whether or not there has been a deliberate intention to deceive or cause confusion on the part of the defendant. If the effect is to cause the goods or services to be passed off as or for those of the plaintiff or to be wrongly connected with the plaintiff then that is usually the end of the matter and the Court is entitled to issue a permanent injunction restraining the defendant from carrying out further acts of passing off and award damages to the plaintiff, including an award of legal costs. Thus, for people in business one of the primary considerations to take into account in any new marketing activity is whether or not the use of a new product packaging, colour scheme, advertising slogan or theme is likely to give rise to a misrepresentation, or at least an uncertainty in the minds of the trade or public, as to where the goods or services emanate. The misrepresentation does not have to be to everyone and even if only a few customers are confused or deceived by, perhaps, not reading product packaging carefully enough, this is often still all that is required to establish a case of passing off.

Examples of passing off

To illustrate the kind of difficulties which can arise when marketing products or services it is useful to look at two cases where passing off was successfully established in the Courts, the first being the 'Jif Lemon' case. As everyone knows, it has been the practice of the owners of the trade mark JIF to sell their lemon juice in a container shaped like a lemon and coloured yellow. Another manufacturer of lemon juice decided to do likewise and even though a different coloured top was used and the product was clearly marked with the name of that manufacturer, the Court nevertheless held that the end result was that a sufficient cross-section of the public purchased the product in the mistaken belief that it was JIF lemon juice, or a variety thereof. A permanent injunction was granted which effectively means that the manufacturers of JIF lemon juice now have a perpetual monopoly in the use of lemon-shaped containers for selling lemon juice, or at least for as long as they retain their exclusive reputation for doing so.

The other case concerned a slogan for selling beefburgers. McDonalds had for many years been selling outsized beefburgers with reference to the trade mark 'Big Mac'. One of their rivals, Burger King, decided to go one better and in their advertising slogans started to use a delicious parody of Big Mac in order to sell its own giant beefburger by stating that it was 'not just Big Mac'. Mcdonalds disapproved of this and were able to establish to the satisfaction of the Court that a sufficiently large cross-section of the public wrongly believed there to be some connection between both products. On this basis the Court granted a permanent injunction restraining Burger King from using the slogan any further. Perhaps this was a rather extreme example but it does, nevertheless, illustrate the dangers of embarking upon expensive advertising campaigns aimed directly against a competitor's products or services without careful consideration of all the issues.

Conclusion

Although originally designed to provide a remedy for what are now often referred to as counterfeiting activities, the law relating to passing off has grown to the extent that it is more akin to the unfair competition laws established in the rest of Europe. As a general rule, it may be considered that any misrepresentation occurring in trade is likely to find a remedy in the United Kingdom through the use of the law relating to passing off.

Copyright

The statutory definition of copyright infringement is quite complex and depends upon the nature of the copyright work involved, when the copyright arose and who owns it. The matter is made more complex as a result of there being two kinds of infringement, with different penalties applicable to each. The first kind is primary infringement which can be viewed as infringement by virtue of the creation of an infringing copy of the copyright work, and the other is secondary infringement, which can be viewed as the exploitation of the results of primary infringement. The manufacturer of a pirate compact disc is guilty of primary infringement and someone who deals in those discs is guilty of secondary infringement. If the manufacturer makes and sells the pirate disc he is guilty of both. Similarly, someone who sings a copyright song in public for purposes of profit at, say, a concert is guilty of primary infringement, whereas the seller of tickets for the concert is guilty of secondary infringement.

Because the law relating to copyright has changed substantially in the last few years, in some ways by clarifying or expanding upon what is meant by copyright and copyright works, and in others by reducing the scope of works previously protected by copyright, this has meant in turn that transitional provisions have had to be invoked in the new legislation to provide a bridge linking the old law to the new. It is therefore beyond the scope or intention of this book to specify all possible definitions of what could constitute infringement of a copyright. This section will therefore outline only the general principles involved and should not be regarded as being exhaustive on the subject.

Definitions of primary infringement

It is convenient to divide the definition as to what constitutes copyright infringement into five general categories and using this scheme we then have the following definitions:

1. Copying the copyright work, which means reproducing the work in any material form. This definition also includes storing the work in any medium by electronic means, such as by the use of cassette tapes and floppy discs. With respect to artistic works which are not purely functional in their nature, reproducing such works in any material form. This also includes making in three dimensions a copy of a two-dimensional work.
2. Issuing copies of a copyright work to the public, such as by way of sale or hire.
3. In respect of a literary, dramatic or musical work, performing the work in public using any mode of visual or acoustic presentation, including by means of a sound recording, film, broadcast, or cable programme of the work. This definition of infringement also includes delivering lectures, public addresses, speeches and sermons.
4. Broadcasting the copyright work, including by means of cable programme service.
5. Making an adaptation of the copyright work which, in relation to literary or dramatic works, means making a translation, or a version of a dramatic work in which it is converted in a non-dramatic work or vice versa, or making a version of the work in which the story or action is conveyed wholly or mainly by means of pictures, such as in a comic strip. In respect of musical works, an adaptation means an arrangement or transcription of the work and in respect of computer programs the adaptation could also include making a version of the program in which it is converted into or out of a computer language or code, or into a different computer language or code.

Definitions of secondary infringement

It is also convenient to divide the definition as to what constitutes secondary copyright infringement into five categories, as follows:

1. Importing an infringing copy of the work into the United Kingdom;
2. Possessing or dealing with an infringing copy such as by way of sale or hire, exhibition or distribution of the copyright work;
3. Providing means specifically designed or adapted for making copies of copyright work, such as making and selling a mould for making an article which would, if made, constitute copyright infringement;
4. Permitting the use of premises for a public performance of a literary, dramatic or musical work in which copyright subsists;

5. Where copyright is infringed by a public performance or the playing or showing of the work in public, the person supplying apparatus or a substantial part of apparatus for playing such sound recordings, showing such films or receiving such visual images or sounds conveyed by electronic means also infringes the copyright.

It is important to note that secondary infringement requires as a prerequisite that the infringer must know or have reason to believe that the acts done would or could constitute infringement of a copyright. Anyone who innocently does something which otherwise would constitute an act of secondary infringement does not infringe. This does not, however, mean that it is simply necessary for such a person to plead innocence of the existence of the copyright in order to escape liability, since the Court is entitled to assume, for example, that a person giving permission for his premises to be used for a public performance of a musical work would have reason to believe that the musical work will be covered by a copyright. Accordingly, the failure by such a person to enquire as to whether permission had being given by the copyright owner to perform the musical work may well be regarded as being unreasonable and simply designed to avoid liability, in which case the Courts are likely to regard the lack of knowledge as being self-imposed for reasons of convenience rather than prudence.

Exceptions

As always, there are exceptions as to what constitutes infringement and these can be summarized as follows:

1. Fair dealing in literary, dramatic, musical or artistic works for the purposes of research or private study.
2. Fair dealing in the work for the purposes of criticism, review and news reporting.
3. Incidental inclusion of a copyright material in an artistic work, sound recording, film, broadcast or cable programme.
4. Acts done for the purposes of education such as performing, playing or showing a copyright work in the course of the normal activities of an educational establishment, and including copying small portions of copyright works solely for the purpose of education.
5. The use of copyright material by libraries and archives, other than the multiple reproduction, i.e. photocopying of copies of material.
6. Acts which are necessary for public administration such as for the purposes of parliamentary or judicial proceedings, Royal Commissions and statutory inquiries, the keeping of public records and other forms of public business.

7. Copying any aspect of the shape or configuration either internally or externally, of the whole or part of an article, drawing, written description or other form of record, unless the design relates to an artistic work in which copyright subsists.
8. Acts done at a time when, or in pursuance of arrangements made at a time when, it is not possible by recent inquiries to ascertain the identity of the owner of the copyright and in the circumstances it is reasonable to assume that either the copyright has expired or the author has died 50 years or more before the beginning of the calendar year in which the act is done or the arrangements are made.

The above list of exceptions as to what constitutes copyright infringement is not exhaustive but nevertheless illustrates the extent to which copyright can impinge upon everyday activities, hence the need for a range of escape routes to liability in respect of acts of which it is not fair or reasonable to complain. Even so, it will be apparent that most of the above list of exceptions to infringement would not normally be directly relevant to a business and thus, as a general rule, the owner of a business would not be able to escape liability for either primary or secondary infringement unless he did not know and had no reason for believing that the acts complained of constituted infringement. It should also be remembered that copyright infringement only occurs after there has been copying. The separate creation of a work which, by coincidence, is similar to another copyright work does not give rise to copyright infringement of the first work and the owner of the second work is entitled to exploit it to the same extent as the owner of the first work.

Design right

As with copyright, there is a two-tier level of infringement of the design right, primary infringement occurring by the act of copying, and secondary infringement occurring by the act of dealing in the infringing copy. Once again, secondary infringement only occurs when the person deals with an article which he knows or has reason to believe is an infringing article.

Definitions of infringement

Primary infringement occurs by:

1. making articles to the design, or
2. making a design document recording the design for the purposes of enabling such articles to be made.

Secondary infringement occurs by:

1. importing an infringing article into the United Kingdom for commercial purposes,
2. possessing the article for commercial purposes, or
3. selling, hiring out, or offering for sale or hire the infringing article in the course of business

Exceptions

The exceptions to infringement of a design right are:

1. Making and using articles for private, non-commercial, use.
2. Where copyright subsists in a work which consists of or includes a design in which a design right also subsists, it is not an infringement of the design right to do anything which would otherwise be an infringement of the copyright in the work. Thus, if the design in question is also covered by a copyright then an action for infringement only lies in respect of the copyright itself, not both. Equally, it means that anyone authorized to utilize a copyright work cannot infringe a design right if part or all of the design in question is included in the copyright work, even if the design right is owned by or licensed to another party.
3. Acts done for the purpose of supplying articles for the services of the Crown relative to the defence of the realm, foreign defence and health service purposes, provided that a government department authorizes such acts.

Conclusion

Hence, infringement of a design right is really very similar to infringement of a registered design, although it must be remembered that it is only possible to register a design which has some artistic quality and is not purely functional, whereas a design right can arise in respect of even purely functional designs unless they are excluded by the 'must fit' and 'must match' exclusions referred to in Chapter 4.

General considerations

The above definitions of which acts constitute infringement and which do not are necessarily greatly condensed. Even so, it will be obvious that except in the most straightforward of cases, professional help must be sought whenever infringement is suspected or alleged. A common mistake is to write to the infringer and demand an end to the infringing activity. In many instances, the mere act of threatening infringement is itself actionable in the Courts, particularly if the alleged infringer establishes that damage is caused to its business or reputation. For any business, the golden rule must always be to keep silent about any contentious issue regarding infringement of an intellectual property right until professional advice has been obtained.

8 Legal and other remedies for infringements

As we saw from the previous chapter, and perhaps not surprisingly given the variety of subjects covered, the definitions as to which acts constitute infringement of intellectual property rights are extensive. Fortunately, having reached the point where infringement has been identified, the legal remedies available are fairly uniform in their application and result, the only notable exceptions being variations in the level of monetary damages obtainable by a successful plaintiff, and the criminal nature of some acts of infringement.

This chapter will deal mainly with civil remedies for infringement since it is primarily by this method that businesses can recoup money lost through infringing activity, and also prevent further acts of infringement. However, the criminal nature of some acts of infringement are important to know about and are discussed towards the end of the chapter.

The High Court

The Civil Courts in the United Kingdom, including those in Scotland which operate under a different legal framework, provide a forum for solving disputes between parties by means of a trial. Taking as an example a trial in the English High Court relating to alleged infringement of an intellectual property right, the procedures are characterized by the complainant, called the plaintiff, issuing through his legal counsel a writ containing brief details, separately detailed in a statement of claim, of the acts complained about and the relief sought. The writ always includes a return date by which the recipient, the defendant, must answer the allegations either by admitting them and thereby submitting to summary judgment by the Court or, as is more usual, by denying the allegations either in whole or in part. If the allegations are denied, this sets the scene for a full trial before a judge who will issue a decision after reviewing written evidence filed into Court by both parties and hearing oral arguments on behalf of each. Once the decision has been rendered the losing party can appeal against the decision in the Court of Appeal (the Inner House of the Court of Sessions in Scotland), which is then the end of the matter unless the matter still in dispute concerns the interpretation or application of a particular point of law.

If, however, a point of law is in dispute then it is possible to appeal to a third and final stage within the British legal system, the House of Lords. This does not mean all members of the House, but a select few who are considered learned enough to pronounce judgment on issues of law including what Parliament meant by words used in the written Acts of Parliament. It should be noted that the House of Lords does not sit to decide in the final instance on disputes relating to issues of fact since the lower Courts are considered competent enough to deal with such matters.

Thus, in any High Court civil action the plaintiff and defendant each has a right to two bites of the cherry, and a third bite might be available if a legal point, which does not relate to the facts in dispute, has to be settled.

The complexities of High Court action

In principle, this system of administering civil law disputes appears to be simple and efficient, but in reality it is not. There are several reasons for this, many of them arising out of the traditional emphasis which the Courts have relied upon, and come to expect, on the use of professional legal advisers to help plaintiffs and defendants. Until very recently, an action for, say, infringement of a patent in the High Court required, at a minimum, the assistance of a patent agent to advise on technical aspects of the invention and the surrounding prior art, a solicitor, because only a solicitor is entitled to represent a client in legal actions before the High Court; and a barrister, because only a barrister can actually appear in the High Court to argue the case. If the case is complex or extremely important for a client, it would be usual to employ a senior barrister who would normally be a Queen's Counsel, in which case the Court then requires that a junior barrister must also be present to assist his more eminent colleague. Again, if one side decides to employ the services of a QC more often than not the other side will do the same to avoid the risk of losing the dispute because of using a less experienced barrister.

Thus, for any contested patent infringement action we then have as many as 10 or 12 professional advisers involved, quite apart from expert witnesses needed to give evidence on technical aspects of the invention and the background technological field. Again, expert witnesses usually come from the ranks of the professionally qualified, such as Fellows of the Royal Society, chartered engineers, members of the Institute of Electrical Engineers and so on, all requiring professional fees in return for their services.

Then there are the Rules of the Supreme Court, a two-volume work of encyclopaedic length setting out the huge number of procedural rules and regulations which must be adhered to for all matters to be heard before the Court. The rules provide a framework by which, theoretically, plaintiff and defendant alike can be treated fairly. But in practice they also provide a mechanism for each party to cause the other as much trouble and expense as possible in the period between issuance of the writ, up to the time when a final judgment is rendered by the Court, and even beyond. By this means, an experienced litigation lawyer can often outmanoeuvre and wear down a less experienced opponent to a point whereby the other party gives in regardless of the merits of the case. It is therefore perhaps not surprising that the majority of such actions before the High Court are settled well before the trial and before justice has been meted out by the Court.

It has been observed, perhaps rather cruelly, that the internal workings of the British legal system for solving civil disputes appear designed solely for the benefit of the judiciary and legal professions, with little regard to the requirements of the litigants themselves.

The Patents County Court

Fortunately, this self-perpetuating state of affairs may be nearing an end, at least in respect of many intellectual property disputes where a more common-sense approach has now been adopted by the formation of a specialist Court run on the more simplistic lines of a County Court. The new Patents County Court is able to resolve patent and design disputes much more efficiently whilst at the same time minimizing opportunities for engaging in tactical warfare between opposing professional advisers. This new Court is located at Wood Green, North London and opened its doors for business in 1989. It has rapidly obtained a reputation for meting out justice at much lower cost than would be the case if actions of the same type were commenced in the High Court. The new Court relies more on written evidence submitted before the trial and less on wordy arguments expounded by articulate advocates at the actual trial. An important feature of the new Court is that it dispenses with the requirement for engaging multiple legal advisors, patent agents to provide technical background information, solicitors to issue and serve writs and deal with the procedural matters before the Court and barristers to argue the case at the trial. It is now even possible for registered patent agents to appear in person in the Court without a solicitor or barrister being present, although this does not mean that potential litigants should lightly dismiss the experience of solicitors and barristers in such circumstances.

Review of the first 100 cases

It has been reported from a review of the first 100 cases handled by the Patents County Court that 21 were settled before the trial, 10 were listed for trial and 8 judgments had been given after a trial. Of the 8 trial cases the average length of each was only 9 1/4 hours and the average time between issuing a writ of summons and the trial itself was only 42 weeks. Unfortunately, perhaps due to workload pressures, the first eight judgments have all been overturned on appeal! Hopefully, this regrettable record will soon end and be regarded as simply a reflection of teething troubles consequential on the setting up of the, radically different, court. Even so, the contrast with the High Court can hardly be more startling. It is not as if the reason for this was due to the litigants being small to medium-sized businesses, since many of the litigants were multinationals such as Procter & Gamble and Sony. Therefore, assuming things will continue in this way the previously frighteningly expensive task of enforcing patents and registered designs against third-party infringers has now become much easier and more affordable.

The powers of the new Court

The new Patents County Court was created by the Copyright, Designs and Patent Act 1988, which specified that the Court would be available to hear disputes relating to patents, and designs. Surprisingly, but perhaps due to political expediency, the Court was not given the power to deal with disputes relating to copyright, trademarks and know-how, which can still only be resolved in the High Court using the cumbersome and more expensive procedures of conventional practice.

The importance of professional advice

It is obvious that, even with the refreshingly common-sense approach adopted by the new Patents County Court, at least theoretically, litigation is best avoided if at all possible, since once started it can be difficult and often expensive to get out of. Despite this, it is a very serious mistake for a business manager to consider avoiding litigation altogether by trying to resolve disputes without recourse to professional advice, such as by making an informal approach to the other party in the hope of resolving the matter amicably. Occasionally, this approach may work but in most instances it will generally only tend to exacerbate the problem, for plaintiff and defendant alike.

Disadvantages of the informal approach

Most alleged infringers of an intellectual property right, apart from the most blatant – such as manufacturers of pirate video tapes – will generally ignore complaints received from anything other than legal sources. In any case, such complaints are more likely to contain incautious statements which can be exploited at a later stage. More importantly, the warning given by an informal approach to a potential infringer can often provide a mechanism for covering up acts of infringement and thus escaping liability. On the other hand, an infringer receiving a formal letter from a solicitor, registered patent agent or registered trade mark agent is much more likely to take the matter seriously and either end the infringing activity or enter into negotiations aimed at settling the dispute.

Another reason why it is better not to exclude professional advice at this very critical point in time is that in some instances the very act of threatening an alleged infringer is itself actionable in the Court, even though the acts complained of may appear to be clear infringements of the intellectual property right. In those circumstances, the recipient of the threats is given the initiative and can commence legal proceedings to prevent further threats, obtain a monetary award in respect of any damage caused to its business as a result of the threats, such as loss of custom, and recover legal costs at the same time.

Thus, a useful rule to adopt is to call in professional help immediately infringing activity is identified or threatened, but enter into litigation only after every other avenue for settlement of the dispute is explored, unless immediate and irreparable damage to the business is being suffered.

Relief available via the Court

The kinds of relief obtainable by an application to the Court can be conveniently split into two categories, interim relief and permanent relief. Interim relief, as it suggests, is temporary in its nature and usually lasts until a final determination of the matters in dispute by the Court after a trial. The variety of relief available to a plaintiff or a defendant is surprisingly wide and sometimes it is even possible to ask the Court to issue an order granting the relief sought without giving the other side the opportunity to be heard or forewarned. This kind of relief is called *ex-parte* because the other party is not involved in the matter. On the other hand, *inter-partes* relief requires that both parties attend the Court and then argue for or against the relief sought, before the Court makes a decision.

Ex-parte relief

Two kinds of *ex-parte* interim relief are of particular significance in relation to disputes concerning intellectual property and both can have serious consequences for the defendant. They are only available where previous conduct of the defendant makes it clear that if warned of impending legal action he is likely to frustrate the process of administering justice by, for example, disposing of infringing articles, destroying documents and transferring assets.

The Anton Piller order

The first and most widely used form of *ex-parte* relief is called the Anton Piller order. It derives its name from the plaintiff in an action where such an order was obtained from the Court for the first time in circumstances where the plaintiff had strong evidence to suggest to the Court that by serving a writ upon the defendant, the defendant was likely to get rid of incriminating evidence of the alleged acts of infringement.

The relief obtainable by means of an Anton Piller Order, which must be executed by a solicitor acting in his capacity as an officer of the Court, can include seizure of goods and documents, delivery up to the custody of the plaintiff's solicitors of customer lists and details of where the goods were obtained. The order will usually also include an injunction restraining the defendant from repeating acts of infringement until the trial, or until a further hearing is held to determine whether the initial order should continue or be set aside and the defendant be allowed to continue his activities until the trial. Failure to comply with any order of the Court amounts to contempt and is punishable by imprisonment, a fine or both.

Nowadays, an Anton Piller order is not easy to get from the Court, possibly because it has been over-used by plaintiffs in the past and the Courts have tended to become increasingly suspicious as to the motives behind requests for such an order. The order is not intended to provide a mechanism for a fishing expedition on the part of the plaintiff but to preserve incriminating evidence for the Court to consider at the trial.

A street vendor selling pirate tapes would be a suitable target for this kind of order since if he were issued with a writ in the normal manner it would first of all be necessary to ascertain the name of the individual concerned, issue and serve the writ upon him/her personally, the matter then going to trial in the normal manner. Obviously, in those circumstances it would be rather unlikely for the vendor to be still at the same location selling the pirate tapes and it would also be unlikely for the tapes to be there or otherwise accessible to the plaintiff. However, if the proposed defendant is an established company then a plaintiff is unlikely to obtain such an Order, the Court taking the view that a defendant is entitled to be assumed innocent until held otherwise.

The Mareva injunction

The second *ex-parte* interim order obtainable from a Court is called a Mareva injunction. Again, the criterion for obtaining this must be based upon a strong suspicion that upon receiving the usual writ from a plaintiff the defendant will dispose of, rather than incriminating evidence, assets by which the plaintiff could be paid. Thus if, say, a dealer in counterfeit goods had amassed a substantial amount of money as a result of his activities, in those circumstances the Court can order that the assets be frozen until the outcome of the trial is known. Whereas Anton Piller orders are almost solely the province of intellectual property disputes, Mareva orders are common to all civil disputes where a transfer of assets by the defendant would leave him unable to pay all or a substantial part of the plaintiff's claim.

Inter-partes interim orders

Inter-partes interim orders of the Court usually seek to prevent one party from doing something or other. In respect of trade mark infringement where a trade mark owner's reputation could be seriously and permanently damaged by the presence on the market of an inferior product sold under the same or a similar mark, the Court is likely to issue an interim injunction against the defendant immediately to put a stop to his activities until the trial. In other instances of infringement, such as those relating to patents, the Court usually takes the view that reputations are not at stake and any damage sustained by the plaintiff is usually quantifiable in terms of money. In those circumstances it would be unusual for a Court to issue an interim injunction restraining a defendant from continuing the acts complained of, unless they had potential consequences unrelated to causing monetary damage, such as in the use of a patented drug where there is a danger to public health if not manufactured correctly, or in the case of a shoddy imitation of a patented toy, the sale of which could affect the reputation of the new product or cause injury to the user.

The risks of interim orders for the plaintiff

Inter-partes and *ex-parte* orders of the Court are necessarily only temporary in their nature and are designed to provide either or both of the litigants with a measure of relief until the full issues are established at trial. However, this is a double-edged sword since, clearly, if a defendant is prevented from selling a product which is alleged to infringe a patent but which the Court after the trial determines does not, the defendant has then suffered loss and damage as a result of the actions of the plaintiff. Such loss and damage must then be paid for by the plaintiff.

Thus, there is always a significant risk associated with obtaining interim injunctions and similar kinds of relief from the Court and only in the most clear-cut of cases is it wise to have recourse to them. That said, it is a fact that most civil disputes, whether relating to intellectual property or otherwise, take several years to be finally determined by the Court. Hence, particularly in cases of alleged trade mark infringement, the obtaining of an interim injunction up to the trial is often the end of the matter since if a defendant is prevented from selling products with reference to a particular trade mark for a number of years, in most instances he will cease use of the trade mark and adopt another one which is less similar to the plaintiff's mark, thus effectively winning the case for the plaintiff. For this reason only the most stubborn of defendants will usually continue to litigate where the first round has already been lost to the plaintiff and an interim injunction issued by the Court.

After the trial

Once the trial is over the Court is entitled to grant relief to the winning party and unless the case is appealed, the relief is permanent in its effect. If the plaintiff wins, the relief will usually be a permanent injunction against the defendant ordering him to stop the infringing activity and not to repeat it. If the order is ignored the defendant is then guilty of contempt. Damages are calculated and an appropriate award is made to the plaintiff, to be paid for by the defendant. Finally, there is usually an order that the legal costs borne by the winning party should be paid by the losing party, although, as mentioned later, this does not mean that all legal costs can be recovered.

Calculation of damages

How an award of damages is calculated depends upon the particular kind of intellectual property but will usually be based upon either of two possible heads, an account of the profits actually earned by the infringer, or the damage (in monetary terms) actually suffered by the plaintiff. For a defendant who wins, obviously there can be no account of profits to claim but the damages sustained can include the loss of opportunity to exploit a market as a result of an injunction having been obtained by the plaintiff up to the trial of the action.

In patent and registered design disputes

In most patent and registered design disputes a successful plaintiff can normally expect to receive, if an account of profits is not elected, damages calculated on a royalty basis as if the infringer had obtained a licence to use the invention or the design from the plaintiff in return for a royalty payment. There is no standard royalty amount and much depends upon the nature of the technology or design, as the case may be. Simple inventions involving only a small improvement over the known art can usually be licensed for between 3 and 6 per cent of the selling price. At the other extreme, if the invention concerns a patented drug, drug companies can usually expect to license the use of such patented technology for around 45 per cent of the selling price of the drug. Little wonder, then, that many hard-fought legal battles for patent infringement involve drug companies.

In trade mark and copyright disputes

Damages claims in respect of infringement of a registered trade mark, or in common law actions for passing off, are not usually based upon a royalty but more on what the defendant has actually earned by the infringing activity, or what the plaintiff has lost. On the other hand, the penalties for infringing copyright depend upon when the copyright arose and when the infringing activity took place. It will be recalled that an important feature of the Copyright, Patents and Design Act 1988 was the abolition of conversion damages for acts of primary infringement, being damages calculated as the actual value of the infringing goods. Infringers of copyrights are now only liable for damages based upon a royalty which would otherwise be obtained for use of the copyright work, generally no more than a few per cent of the selling price of the article, with the exception of audio and video tapes and discs where a 30 per cent royalty is not unusual in the music and film industry.

Legal costs

It was stated earlier that the winning party is usually entitled to his legal costs, but this is misleading since in most cases the Court will normally only award about a half to two-thirds of the actual costs expended in any particular case. A trial costing several hundred thousand pounds can therefore still leave a winning party substantially out of pocket, particularly if the winning party is the defendant with no counterclaim against the plaintiff. Therefore, unless the less expensive, but still not insignificantly so, Patents County Court is used as a forum for settling the dispute, it is necessary for litigants to plan carefully for, first, the requirement to pay legal fees at regular intervals during the course of the litigation and, second, the possibility of having to pay out a substantial sum of money if the Court finds in favour of the other party. Sometimes, well-advised defendants will put aside a percentage of profits being earned by the alleged infringing activity while the case is pending before the Court to provide for the possibility of losing at the end of the day.

Criminal infringement

It was mentioned earlier that some acts of infringement of intellectual property rights are in fact criminal in their nature and thus subject to criminal penalties including fines and imprisonment. Such offences can occur in respect of infringement of copyright and infringement of registered trade marks. Infringement of patents and registered designs, passing off and breaches of confidential know-how continue to be solely actionable by means of civil litigation. Why Parliament has chosen to single out infringers of copyright and trade marks for potentially criminal punishment is not clear but is perhaps based upon the view that dealers in pirate tapes or counterfeit watches bearing a forged trade mark are criminal in their character and therefore it is appropriate to apply criminal sanctions.

Copyright

A person becomes liable to criminal proceedings in relation to infringement of a copyright if that person knowingly infringes the copyright by manufacturing and selling articles made as a direct result of copying. Note that the infringer must know that what he is doing constitutes copyright infringement and there must also be monetary gain. Upon summary conviction before a magistrate a person convicted can be subjected to a fine not exceeding £1000 and a prison term not in excess of 12 months. If the infringing activity is carried out by a company, rather than by an individual, then directors of the company could also be held personally liable for criminal acts carried out under their direction by the company.

Trade marks

In connection with the forging of trade marks, similar considerations apply, those convicted being subject to a fine not exceeding £1000 and again imprisonment for a maximum of 12 months. However, the definition of what constitutes forging a trade mark is much narrower than the definition of what constitutes infringement of a trade mark under the civil law. Forging a trade mark means actually copying it in its entirety and applying it to a product for sale, if used as a trade mark for goods, or using it in relation to the provision of a service in the expectation of receiving a monetary or other reward. Again, directors of a company can be held liable, provided they know that what they sanction the company to do amounts to the forgery of someone else's trade mark.

Involvement of police and customs officers

Because some acts of copying a copyright work or forging a trade mark are actionable under the criminal law they are now of interest to police and customs and excise officers. This is not to say that it is now only possible for a person to allege an infringement of a copyright or a trade mark in order to enlist the help of such officers but, on the other hand, if clear acts of blatant copying or forging of a trade mark come to light an alternative to an expensive civil action may well be an approach to the police or the Customs and Excise Office with a request that criminal proceedings be instituted. This is likely to be particularly useful for dealing with street vendors and suchlike but can also be extremely effective in respect of organized counterfeiting businesses. Needless to say, pursuing the criminal case against a party does not, in any way, prevent a plaintiff from commencing a civil action and hence seeking a monetary or other award in respect of damages suffered.

Conclusion

In this chapter we have briefly reviewed various legal remedies for dealing with acts of infringement of intellectual property rights and some suggestions have been made as to how to proceed once an infringement has been identified. In the next chapter, we will deal with the equally important topic of avoiding litigation or criminal sanctions by avoiding infringing intellectual property rights in the first place.

9 Avoiding infringement problems through clearance searches

The recipient of a lawsuit alleging infringement of an intellectual property right usually knows that he has made a mistake somewhere along the line and that in hindsight the lawsuit could have been avoided. Obviously, for those who knowingly engage in infringing activities at the expense of the owner of the intellectual property right the solution lies in their own hands, and it is not the intention of this chapter to suggest avenues of escape from liability for such persons. Most disputes concerning intellectual property arise out of ignorance of the rights of other parties and, particularly, out of ignorance of the law. Sometimes the person accused of infringing is completely unaware of the existence of the intellectual property right, but in other instances it may be a case of having taken a gamble on, for example, making a similar but not identical product to that of a successful competitor, using a similar but not identical trade mark, or even using similar but not identical packaging. In some instances the gamble pays off, but in many instances it does not, particularly where the owner of the intellectual property right is familiar with the legal issues and remedies available, or adopts an aggressive stance towards competition.

Examples of avoidable litigation

This chapter identifies areas where uncertainty can be avoided in order to lessen the possibility of litigation being commenced by, usually, a competitor. It is, of course, never possible to eliminate the risk of litigation entirely but it most definitely is possible to reduce this risk considerably by careful planning.

Monopoly right

At its most extreme, a monopoly right in respect of a registered trade mark, registered design or a patent can eliminate competition. To illustrate by way of a particular example relating to a claim for patent infringement in the United States, Polaroid Corporation, which owns a number of patents relating to instant film technology and instant film cameras, was, after a legal battle lasting several years and costing millions of dollars, successful in completely eliminating from the market a competing range of films and cameras marketed by The Eastman Kodak Company. The defendant in that action had argued that either the patents were invalid or not infringed and thus took a gamble which ultimately did not pay off. The damages and related monetary awards given to Polaroid Corporation exceeded US$900 million, although they were expecting an award of several billion US dollars. To illustrate further the significance of that litigation to both parties, after the size of the monetary award was announced by the Court the price of Polaroid stock actually fell whereas the price of Kodak stock rose sharply! Shareholders in both companies had anticipated a higher award of damages which, in turn, was reflected in the share price of each at the time the Court announced the size of the award. It is to Kodak's credit that the underlying strength of their other business activities enabled them to shrug off the effects of a loss of part of its business and a substantial monetary payment, but it will be apparent that less robust businesses could well have folded.

A new trade mark and packaging

It is not only technology-related intellectual property rights that can give rise to such spectacular consequences for the losing party. A successful copyright claim can spell the end for a one-product company if the product is found to be an infringement of a copyright. Similarly, the marketing of a new product under a new trade mark or with new packaging can give rise to the loss of several months' potential business if a third party obtains an interim injunction restraining use of the mark or packaging until a trial is held to determine whether it is too similar to that used by the plaintiff. As mentioned in the previous chapter, in circumstances such as this a new trade mark or a new packaging style will usually be adopted as soon as possible since, above all, a business must sell its wares or services in order to survive. Getting the newly named product back onto the market after a delay of even only a few months can often have serious consequences for all but the most substantial of businesses.

Professional help

The best advice for avoiding problems of this nature is to seek professional advice before any new product or service is put onto the market and, preferably, even before money has been spent on formulating marketing strategies. The cost of asking a trade mark agent to determine if a particular trade mark or packaging style would be considered too similar to that of a competitor is insignificant compared to the cost of preparing a product or service for market, and is the only way in which a responsible decision can be made by a business on whether to proceed or choose another name for the product or service.

The launch of every new product or every newly named product or service onto the market necessarily brings with it the risk of infringing someone's rights and hence, for a company to proceed without obtaining professional advice beforehand is little short of negligent. Unfortunately, lessons are more often learned through experience rather than foresight, perhaps because of the opposing philosophies of, on the one hand, marketing considerations and, on the other, the cautious approach needed to avoid problems with intellectual property. This is not to say that marketing, as an activity, is necessarily an incautious one, but merely to recognize the fact that marketing means selling a product or a service at the expense of competitors which, roughly translated, often means adopting aggressive and bold tactics to outsell and outperform them. This chapter does not seek to alter such philosophies, but merely to suggest ways in which, with a little forethought and expenditure a large proportion of the potential problems associated with marketing can be eliminated or at least minimized.

Patents

Patents only last for a maximum of 20 years from the date of filing which means that it is only the manufacture or use of relatively new products or processes which can infringe a patent. As mentioned in Chapter 2, patents can be granted for surprisingly modest improvements in products or processes, and several patents owned by different parties can exist, each covering different parts of the same product or process. This means that manufacturing or selling relatively new products or using relatively new processes or products obtained by such processes can often mean running into trouble with patents owned by third parties. Obviously, if a company has been using a process or making and selling a product for several years without problems arising this is a strong indicator that no relevant patent exists but where a new process is to be used or a new product is to be made and sold, it is prudent to find out if patent rights exist which could cause problems later on.

Discovering if patent rights exist

This is achieved by carrying out patent clearance searches, which are highly specialized in their nature and although they can be done by anyone with sufficient time to spend at the Patent Office, or in one of the several major reference libraries in the United Kingdom where patent literature is stored, they are best left to the professional patent searchers.

Most firms of patent agents will be able to carry out searches, or at least provide names of companies which specialize in this type of activity. The cost is not great and for an everyday item such as a new type of can-opener, a thorough search of UK patents relating to can-opener technology is likely to cost under £1,000. This is an insignificant amount compared to the cost of manufacturing and marketing the product and well worth spending, even if it is felt likely that no patent rights exist. It will also be recalled from Chapter 7 that in some instances it is possible to avoid the consequences of patent infringement if the infringement is innocent. But that innocence requires as a prerequisite a reasonable amount of inquiry beforehand. Failure to carry out a patent infringement search prior to making a new product automatically excludes the possibility of a defendant hiding behind a defence based upon innocence.

The scope of the patent's claims

A patent infringement search often reveals a number of possibly relevant patents in any given area of technology and great care must be taken to avoid assuming that any particular patent is not infringed simply by referring to the drawings or what is written in the accompanying description. Infringement is established by reference to the claims, but there are other influencing factors which make the interpretation of the claims a specialist task. Generally speaking, it is only chartered patent agents who are capable of providing an assessment as to whether or not a particular patent claim is likely to be infringed. As well as commissioning a patent infringement search, considertion should therefore be given to requesting a chartered patent agent's opinion as to infringement. Even if this increases the costs twofold, the amount is still relatively insignificant and, in any event, the information will provide a sound basis upon which to make a decision as to whether or not to proceed. Of course, an opinion is just an opinion and the Court may take a different view, but an opinion based upon years of technical and legal training together with everyday experience can usually be relied upon.

Obtaining up-to-date information

There is another significant advantage to carrying out patent infringement searches prior to the launch of a new product or process and this stems from the fact that a patent is only granted in return for disclosure of the new technical advance in the art. It follows from this principle that patent searching can also be used as a means of learning of advances in the art which have been made fairly recently. Most large companies engaged in developing new products and processes take advantage of this fact as a short cut for research and development by finding out what their competitors are up to and, sometimes, perceiving ways of improving newly developed products and processes which may not have already occurred to the competitor. Needless to say, this can provide a springboard for a company to bypass the competition and, at the same time, to design around, if that is at all possible, any existing patents. However, at the risk of overemphasizing the point, for every successful plaintiff in a patent infringement action is a defendant who could or should have avoided the consequences with recourse to professional advice at an early stage.

Registered designs

The firms of patent agents or specialist companies who carry out patent infringement searches also provide similar services in respect of registered designs, although such searching is not nearly so complex. This is because designs are relatively easy to classify into particular kinds of products and there are many fewer registered designs at any given time than there are in-force patents. This is reflected in the cost of a design infringement search which is usually about half that of a patent search and, similarly, an opinion from a patent agent as to whether or not a particular design infringes a registered design is usually correspondingly cheaper.

It must also be remembered that to register a design it only has to be new and have some artistic quality so that trends in fashion tend to be reflected in the number and variety of registered designs filed most recently. Registered designs can therefore also provide a rich source of suggestions for any business to acquire, for free, starting-point suggestions for developing newly designed products.

Trade marks

Problems with patents are avoided by not making use of the technology recited in the patent claims of each patent and, similarly, avoiding problems with registered designs simply means not making or selling products which are the same or substantially the same as the registered design. However, because there is a different definition as to what constitutes infringement of a trade mark, this is perhaps the most problematic area of intellectual property when it comes to trying to avoid problems with other trade mark owners. The reason is that infringement of a registered trade mark is defined as being use by another person of the same or a confusingly similar trade mark in respect of the same goods or services for which the mark is registered. Similarly, in a passing-off action, the plaintiff essentially has to satisfy the Court that the defendant's use of the same or a similar mark causes confusion, or is likely to if use of the mark has not yet started. However, what is confusingly similar to one person may not be to another and the history of trade mark litigation is littered with what can be described as occasionally bizarre decisions due to, in the end, the Court (meaning the judge) deciding that there is or is not confusing similarity. The following examples illustrate this possible confusion:

- The mark RYSTA was held by the House of Lords to be confusingly similar to the mark ARISTOC, registered in respect of ladies stockings. Although it may not be immediately apparent why the marks were considered similar, Counsel for Aristoc Ltd had argued during the trial that the mark RYSTA could be pronounced in two ways, one being as in RISSTA and therefore customers asking for an ARISTOC stocking might somehow become confused.
- In another case which again went all the way to the House of Lords, use of the mark BALI was held to be an infringement of the mark BERLEI, registered in respect of brassieres.
- The owners of the mark PLIX obtained an injunction preventing use of PALEXA in respect of toilet preparation.
- The use of WELLS WHIP in respect of ice cream was prevented by the owners of the marks WALLS and WALLS SUPERWHIP, it being held that WALLS and WELLS were confusingly similar.
- An injunction preventing further use of HANDI HANKI was granted, it being held that use of the mark on paper handkerchiefs would be likely to deceive and cause confusion in view of the existing mark HANDY ANDIES.
- PEM BOOKS was held to be too similar to PAN BOOKS and an injunction granted preventing its further use.

These examples are not provided in order to criticize decisions handed down by the Courts (some of the decisions above were overturned on appeal) but to illustrate just how easy it is for wrong assumptions to be made with often disastrous consequences. Trade marks, in their many forms, are the most valuable marketing tools available and choosing a new trade mark requires careful thought from two perspectives, one being market appeal and the other being legal appeal. It is often the case that large sums of money are wasted by carrying out market surveys to determine if a new mark has appeal to the consumer and only then proceeding to check, if at all, if the mark is available for use and if the same mark or a similar one has not already been registered by someone else in respect of the same or similar goods or services.

Today's searches

Nowadays, with the advent of international trade mark databases and very sophisticated computerized searching techniques, there is no excuse for any business to commence marketing a new product or service under a new mark without first checking to see if the coast is clear in all countries where the goods or services are to be traded. Before computer-based searching facilities became widely available, such clearance searches had to be done manually in each country by checking through the records of registered trade marks and this necessarily took quite a long time – it was often several weeks before the results came to hand. However, a comprehensive clearance search can now be undertaken in a great many countries and the results obtained, usually including an opinion from a registered trade mark agent on the relevance of any marks found in the search, in just a few days and at relatively modest cost.

Selecting a new mark

It therefore follows that the selection and searching of new marks for possible use in a business may be achieved more economically by providing a short list of marks arranged in order of preference and then arranging for clearance searches to be done in the required territories starting from the top of the list and working down until one or two are found which appear to be free for use. Having thus established which marks could be used in the chosen territories a market survey could then be used to decide which of the eligible marks is best from a market appeal standpoint.

Registration

Having chosen the mark to be used the next thing is to apply to register it in at least one of the territories where the goods or services are to be traded. Due to the existence of the Paris Convention (discussed at the end of Chapter 1) it will be recalled, UK membership of the convention allows UK individuals and companies to apply to register a mark at the Trade Marks Registry and to then enjoy a right of priority for any later filed trade mark applications in all other countries which are members of the convention, meaning most of the world with the notable exception of Thailand and Taiwan. Thus, filing a trade mark application in the United Kingdom then secures the option to file corresponding applications in other territories within the six-month period allowed, thereby avoiding the possibility of someone else applying to register the same mark or a similar one in an important territory which has only just been searched for possibly conflicting marks.

Avoiding problems in selecting new trade marks therefore means more than simply checking to see if the same or a similar mark is already registered for the relevant area of business and requires positive action to secure legal title to the new trade mark, which inevitably means applying for registration in all territories of interest.

Trade marks in use but not registered

A final point to consider is that although trade mark clearance searches are particularly important they usually only cover marks which have been previously registered or applied for registration and not those marks which may be in use but are not registered. In many countries this is no problem since trade mark rights are only granted through a registration process on a 'first to file' basis. Notable exceptions are the United Kingdom and other Commonwealth countries, Ireland and the United States, which all recognize trade mark ownership rights based upon common law principles of first use in preference to first registration. Since it is not mandatory to register trade marks in these countries, problems can still be encountered even if clearance searches have been carried out before a new mark is used.

Even so, such an additional risk can be minimized by checking through trade directories and similar kinds of publications in each country where common law rights may exist, although it will be understood that having such checks made will increase the cost and time taken for the clearance search to be completed. Fortunately, however, most people recognize the advantage of registering their trade marks and perhaps for this reason clearance searches are usually only limited to searching the Trade Marks Registry in each country of interest. It is also usually the case that when a new mark is chosen, the company or business wishing to adopt it will generally be familiar with other marks used in the same business by competitors, at least in the countries where the business operates, so that although the common law countries do present a problem for those wishing to adopt new marks, normally clearance searches are limited to the Trade Mark Registers and in most cases this is sufficient.

Copyright and the design right

Since there is no facility to register copyright and the new design right in the United Kingdom, or indeed in most other countries of the world, it follows that clearance searches are not possible. In any event, since these forms of intellectual property are not monopolistic in their nature avoiding problems with them is extremely easy. To infringe a copyright or a design right, copying has to occur. A person either has or has not copied something. If there has been no copying then there cannot be any copyright infringement.

Even so, problems can occur when, for example, a manufacturer has seen a new style of product and sets about trying to emulate the design, without copying it exactly. In those circumstances it is usually not sufficient to point to detailed differences between the two designs since the Court will look, instead, at the overall impression given by each and if they are considered to be 'substantially similar' then copyright infringement will have occurred. Accordingly, if there is any doubt as to the origin of any new work which could be covered by copyright it is much safer to seek a legal opinion before going into production. Of course, any legal opinion is just that and cannot guarantee that problems will be avoided but the advantage of seeking an opinion before production commences is that, if the opinion is adverse, nevertheless suggestions could be made as to how to lessen the risk of action being taken by the copyright owner, such as by making further alterations to the product.

Conclusion

Because the subject of intellectual property is so wide ranging any new business activity is potentially affected by it. This chapter has hopefully provided sufficient insight to show that it is relatively easy to avoid problems with intellectual property rights or, put another way, to avoid being a defendant in a lawsuit.

10 Buying and selling intellectual property rights

Avoiding problems with intellectual property rights owned by third parties or exploiting such rights can also be achieved by purchasing them or by taking a licence under the right in return for payment of a royalty fee. This chapter shows how the various forms of intellectual property are bought and sold with attention focused primarily on trade mark rights which, as a form of property, are probably unique.

Ascertaining ownership

As with any proposed purchase, the prudent purchaser first of all checks to see that the vendor owns the property in the first place and is free to sell it. Ownership of patent, registered design and registered trade mark rights is easy to check with reference to, respectively, the records of the Patent Office, the Designs Registry and the Trade Marks Registry. Corresponding checks can be made in other countries if necessary. Checking ownership of copyrights is more problematical since, except in the United States there is no registration procedure and it is therefore usually necessary to rely upon assurances given by the vendor which should always form part of a written sale and purchase agreement, preferably drawn up by a solicitor who would be able to insert in the document clauses to safeguard the purchaser's position.

Transfer of ownership

When intellectual property is transferred from one party to another it is called an assignment of rights. Under general legal principles operating in the United Kingdom transfer of ownership of a property from one party to another can only be achieved in two ways, the first and the most obvious being in return for payment. The payment of money is called the consideration for the assignment and once it is paid the purchaser owns the property. However, sometimes it is desirable to transfer ownership of an intellectual property right from one party to another with no consideration payable, for example, when transferring assets within a group of companies. In those circumstances a transfer can still be made by entering into a Deed of Assignment by which the company owning the intellectual property right, the assignor, transfers all of its rights in the property to the other party, the assignee. The Memorandum and Articles of Association of the company almost always require that any Deed may only be executed by at least two officials of the company, usually either two of the directors or a director and the company secretary. Accordingly, it is often worth while checking the signatories of any assignment document, including an assignment made for a consideration, to ensure that those signing on behalf of the assignor are authorized to do so.

Because intellectual property rights are intangible it follows that payment of money or transfer by deed can give rise to uncertainty as to what has actually been transferred. For example, the owner of a patent may wish to sell it for a sum of money and when the assignment is made what rights does the assignee have? In particular, if it is a UK patent he has purchased, is he entitled to sue a third-party infringer for back-damages prior to the date when he acquired ownership of the patent? If it is a relatively recent patent, is the owner entitled to register it in some of the present and former British overseas dependent territories such as Hong Kong and Singapore, and therefore acquire further property rights in connection with the invention? For these and other reasons, buying and selling intellectual property rights usually requires a great deal of specificity in the assignment document, bearing in mind that the ultimate purpose in purchasing the right is to assert it if necessary in Court against a third-party infringer. There must be no room for doubt as to what has been transferred.

Legal title

Additionally, since patents, registered designs and registered trade marks are State-granted rights it will be apparent that legal title does not pass simply by virtue of the assignor assigning the right to the assignee. When that happens the assignee is said to have a beneficial title in the right but does not have legal title until the transfer has been recorded at, respectively, the Patent Office, Designs Registry or Trade Marks Registry.

It is not mandatory to record a transfer in title, but if action is to be taken against a third-party infringer based only upon beneficial title this can prove problematic; and whilst litigation can still be commenced nevertheless this must always be accompanied by an application to record the change in title. The cost of recordal is quite modest and there is nothing to be gained by not doing so immediately upon transfer of the patent, registered design or registered trade mark, as the case may be.

New owners

However, in order to encourage the new owners of patents to record their legal title the law provides that failure to do so may eventually mean loss of the entire property right if the original vendor purports to sell the same patent or registered design to another party and that other party applies to record the assignment first. In those circumstances, whilst obviously the original purchaser would have a cause of action against the vendor, he does not have a cause of action against the newly registered owner who becomes entitled to the full benefit of the patent or registered design. Whilst such a situation would be unlikely to arise, nevertheless it is built into the law for a purpose and should not be ignored. As well, failure to record the title in a patent excludes the owner from being awarded damages for infringement until such time as the legal ownership has been recorded.

Conflicting rights

The owner of a registered trade mark cannot be sued by the owner of another registered trade mark for infringement and therefore once title in a trade mark has been checked and the sale completed, there is usually nothing further to worry about. However, the same may not be true in respect of patents and registered designs because, as observed earlier in this book, the monopoly granted by the State is not the exclusive right to use the patented invention or registered design, but the right to exclude others from doing so.

Patents and registered designs: the example of television

Particularly in the case of patents, most of which concern improvements over existing products or processes, there is a distinct risk that an earlier patent may still be in force which covers a broader concept such that use of the later patented invention may infringe the earlier patent. For example, if television had been invented just a few years ago then the inventor could still have in force a patent covering the general concept of an electrically operated moving picture display device (the television set) comprising an evacuated glass picture tube having on the inner surface of one end a phosphor coating which can be illuminated when electrons are fired at it from the other end of the tube so that when the electrons are scanned sequentially over the entire surface of the viewing end a picture can be made to appear in accordance with the amount of electrons fired at different parts of the picture tube during each cycle. This is the general principle by which a conventional black and white television works but obviously it can be improved by using three different electron sources and three coatings on the inside of the tube, each representing the primary colours of red, yellow and blue. Using this scheme, the television set can be made to operate in colour and since it is a non-obvious improvement over the black and white version, a patent can be obtained for the system.

In such circumstances, the owner of a patent for the basic concept of television could still prevent manufacture, use and sale of colour television sets because they still fall within the general basic concept which is covered by the first patent. He cannot, however, make and sell colour television sets, because that technology is covered by the second patent.

It will be seen from this hypothetical example that checking the legal ownership of a patent, and to a lesser extent a registered design, may not be enough since there can still be uncertainty as to whether or not the patented invention or the registered design could be used without the risk of infringing third-party rights. A check therefore needs to be made as to whether use of the invention or the design would infringe earlier granted patents or registered designs owned by third parties. Since patents can last for up to 20 years this means that many in-force patents usually exist in most areas of technology and a thorough check can take several weeks. As a practical matter, however, if the invention or design has been publicly used by the assignor prior to the sale for a reasonable length of time and no action has been taken by a third party then this is usually a good indicator that no conflicting rights exist. Even where the invention or design is relatively new, if the assignor has been intimately involved in the area of business concerned for some years then he can usually be relied upon to provide some measure of assurance that no third-party rights exist. However, it is never possible to be absolutely sure of this and it is perhaps for this reason that many assignments of intellectual property do not contain absolute warranties as to the validity of the property right being transferred or the ability of the assignee to continue to exploit the rights after the sale has been completed.

Trade marks – a special case

Turning now to trade marks, it was stated earlier in this chapter that as items of property they are unique. This is because trade marks function at their most basic level as business identifiers, at least to the extent of indicating that a product or service is of a particular quality or comes from a particular source, which is usually the trade mark owner. Selling a trade mark therefore brings with it a risk of confusion or deception arising in the minds of the public. For this reason there are strict rules which must be adhered to if a trade mark is to be validly transferred from one party to another. Obviously, if a trade mark has not been used but is simply registered, there is little or no risk of public deception arising by virtue of transfer of ownership. The problem arises when the mark has been used and the law attempts to minimize the risk of confusion arising in a rather artificial and complicated manner by introducing into the law the concept of 'goodwill' and then, having done so, using this as a means to regulate the transfer of trade marks. Ultimately, the objective is not achieved in the manner in which the law perceives but, as will be seen later, usually by practical common sense on the part of the purchaser.

Goodwill

As everyone knows, the goodwill of a business is the attractive force which brings customers back time and time again. Customers may return because they like the quality of the goods or the services offered, the price, the location and even the politeness of the staff. If the business has many branches, such as a retail store chain, then customers are just as likely to frequent other stores at different locations so that the goodwill pervades the entire operation. To identify each store in the chain a business identifier must necessarily be used, the business identifier being of course the trade mark of the business. Thus, once a trade mark is in use it is inextricably linked with the goodwill of the business since, necessarily, it identifies the business in which goodwill is enjoyed. It therefore follows that if a trade mark is sold there is always the risk that goods or services of an inferior quality may be provided by the new owner, although, usually, the new owner is prudent enough to appreciate this simple concept and ensures that the quality is maintained.

Transfer without goodwill

The law attempts to tackle this problem by imposing on all owners of registered trade marks who use their marks two basic conditions permitting their valid transfer. The first is that if the mark is sold without the goodwill of the business then under the direction of the Trade Marks Registry the fact of assignment must be advertised in newspapers and relevant trade journals so that the general public and the trade are warned that a sale of the trade mark has been made. On its face, this requirement seems sensible, but only if it is accepted that a trade mark which has been used can be so artificially separated from the goodwill attaching to it. There is, however, considerable doubt as to how goodwill can still exist when a trade mark which formerly identified the products or services has been transferred to another party. Even so, the fact that an assignment without the goodwill is publicized does at least serve the function of warning the trade and public as to precisely what has occurred, except for the fact that the Trade Marks Registry only require advertisement of the registration number of the trade mark and not the trade mark itself! It is difficult to see how a statement in a newspaper to the effect that a trade mark registration number has been sold can have any practical meaning.

Transfer with goodwill

Many trade marks which are in use at the time of sale are assigned with the whole of the goodwill of the business and in these circumstances the law does not require any advertisement of the fact of the assignment to be made. The rationale behind this is also difficult to understand since if it is necessary to advertise an assignment of a trade mark without the goodwill, then it would seem to be even more appropriate to advertise an assignment of a trade mark with the goodwill, if the object of the exercise is to avoid deception or confusion arising by alerting the trade and public to the fact that there has been change of ownership in the business identifier.

Transfer of partial goodwill

From the foregoing, it will be seen that the valid transfer of trade mark rights must necessarily also include a conscious decision on whether to transfer the goodwill in the mark. However, what often happens is that a trade mark is assigned only with the goodwill symbolized by it rather than the whole of the goodwill of the business, particularly if the business owns many trade marks. When this happens the assignment is considered, in law, to be an assignment with only part of the goodwill of the business and is therefore treated in the same manner as an assignment made without any goodwill at all, so that the fact of assignment has to be publicized if the mark is in use at the time of transfer.

Time span

The law makes it mandatory that an application must be made to the Trade Marks Registry for directions to advertise the fact of the assignment of a registered trade mark without the entire goodwill of the business within six months of the date of the assignment document, or within any further period which the Trade Marks Registry may allow, otherwise any such assignment is effectively invalid.

11 Licensing and franchising

The owner of an intellectual property right can exploit it either directly or by allowing others to do so, much as a home owner can either choose to live in the house or let others do so in return for rental income. Those who choose not to rent out the intellectual property right to others often enjoy a monopoly right, just as the Polaroid Corporation did in respect of its instant film and camera technology, referred to in Chapter 9.

Royalties

The alternative is to allow others to have a licence to exploit the intellectual property right in return for a royalty, usually calculated as a percentage of the net selling price of the end product. The royalty percentage is calculated having regard to the value of the intellectual property right being licensed and can be as high as 50 per cent or 60 per cent for patented pharmaceutical drugs, or as low as 1 or 2 per cent if the patented technology constitutes only a small component of an everyday product. The royalty calculation is almost always based on what the market will bear and if, for example, the owner of a registered design for a newly shaped table lamp wishes to license the right to utilize the design to third parties then the royalty is usually calculated on the basis that the new design is likely to sell better than existing designs, but is not likely to render existing designs entirely obsolete. Thus, if it is a really good design likely to attract good sales then a 5 per cent or even 10 per cent royalty may be expected but if the design is only a relatively minor improvement over existing designs then a correspondingly lower royalty can be anticipated.

Licensing

The person owning an intellectual property right who decides to license it to another party is called the licensor and the recipient of the licence is called the licensee. There are three main kinds of licence, these being exclusive, non-exclusive and sole licences.

Exclusive licences

An exclusive licence means just that, i.e. it excludes everyone else including the owner of the intellectual property right from exploiting it. If the right is in respect of a patented invention then the owner of an exclusive licence is usually permitted to enforce the right against others to ensure that an effective monopoly is maintained for the duration of the licence. Similarly, an exclusive licensee of a trade mark is the only one entitled to put the trade mark on the goods or to use the trade marks in relation to the services provided, as the case may be. Naturally enough, an exclusive licensee expects to pay more for the privilege of exclusivity than a non-exclusive or sole licensee and this usually means a higher royalty payable to the licensor. This is often coupled with sales performance requirements to ensure that the licensor receives a minimum level of royalties per year.

The advantage to the licensor granting an exclusive licence is that, once the intellectual property right has been established, little more has to be done except monitor the performance of the licensee and receive the resulting income. Equally, the licensee is in a better position to dictate how marketing is to be conducted and the only other consideration he must worry about is whether any minimum target levels are or will be achieved.

Non-exclusive licences

Non-exclusive licences mean that the intellectual property right is being shared with others and because of this there is competition to deal with. Often, patented technology is licensed non-exclusively to competitors in the same industry who all pay the same level of royalty to the patentee. The patentee then not only reaps the profit of the royalties earned but, if he is in the same industry, he can also sell his products either at the same price as the competition and enjoy a higher profit margin, or at a correspondingly reduced price to earn about the same per unit level of profit as the competition. However, by doing the latter the patentee probably enjoys a higher volume of sales in view of the lower cost to the consumer of the product.

Sole licences

A sole licence means that only one licence has been granted and no other licences will be, but the licensor nevertheless retains the right to exploit the intellectual property on his own behalf. Since this is a situation between exclusive and non-exclusive licensing the royalties obtainable also lie somewhere between the two although, not surprisingly, this form of licence is not very popular since it still leaves the licensee in competition with the licensor, at least theoretically so.

Determining ownership of a licenced intellectual property

Taking a licence from the owner of an intellectual property right should be viewed no differently from purchasing the right itself and it therefore follows that checks should be made to ensure that what is being licensed is owned by the licensor and, more importantly, is free to be exploited by the licensee. If the subject of the licence is a registered design and the licensee produces articles in accordance with the design and then sells them but is sued for infringement, it is no defence to say that permission had been given by the licensor. Similarly, the licensor is not liable in law for the infringement. In the circumstances, at best, the licensee may be in a position to sue the licensor although most licences will usually include a safety clause for the licensor specifically denying liability in respect of any acts done under the licence which may infringe third-party rights.

Compulsory licences

Although licensing of intellectual property is generally a voluntary matter on the part of the licensor, in some instances a third party can obtain a licence either compulsorily or as of right, meaning that a licence cannot be refused if requested.

Compulsory licences can be obtained in respect of a patent and a registered design if the owner of the right either does not, or does not sufficiently exploit the property. This 'working' requirement is three years after grant for a patent and at any time after grant for a registered design. It is intended to prevent owners of inventions and designs from stifling industry by sitting on inventions or designs which others wish to exploit and to encourage investment in new products and processes, thereby helping the economy.

Grounds for obtaining a compulsory licence

An application for a compulsory licence under a patent can be made to the comptroller of the Patent Office on any of the following grounds:

1. The invention is not being worked in the United Kingdom, or not to the fullest extent reasonably possible.
2. If the invention concerns a product, a demand for the product is not being met in the United Kingdom on reasonable terms or is being met substantially through importation.

3. Importation of a product or a product obtained by means of a process is causing the patented invention not to be commercially worked in the United Kingdom.
4. Because of the refusal of the proprietor of the patent to grant a licence on reasonable terms, a market for the export of any patented product made in the United Kingdom is not being supplied, or the working of another patented invention which makes a substantial contribution to the technological art is being prevented or hindered, or development of commercial or industrial activities is being unfairly prejudiced.
5. Because of adverse conditions imposed by the patentee on the granting of licences under the patent the establishment or development of commercial or industrial activities in the United Kingdom are being unfairly prejudiced.

From the above it will be apparent that the compulsory licensing provisions are really aimed at ensuring that the existence of patents or registered designs does not hinder the economic development of the United Kingdom. Therefore, the working requirements represent a very serious derogation from the otherwise monopolistic right enjoyed, such as by a patentee over the use of the patented technology.

Compulsory licensing and the EEC

Whilst it must be right that the owner of a broad patent covering a brand new area of technology should not be in a position to stifle the exploitation by others of improvements or refinements to the technology, nevertheless it is questionable as to how the remainder of the law fits in with EEC law, which is built on the premiss that all member states will treat each other equally.

It has already been held by the European Commission that the compulsory licensing provisions are for the most part discriminatory against other member states of the EEC and may well not be legally enforceable, particularly since other member states do not have such working requirements. The discrimination arises, of course, when the market for a particular product is being supplied by a company based in another member state of the EEC, who may own patent rights covering all countries of the EEC. In these circumstances, whilst UK law currently allows a third party the opportunity to obtain a licence and thus compete with the patentee, provided the new product is to be manufactured in the United Kingdom, there is a clear conflict with European Community law.

Refusal of applications for compulsory licences

Although UK law allows for compulsory licensing at any time after three years from the grant of a patent, if the patented invention is not being commercially worked or not being worked to the fullest extent which is reasonably practicable, this does not mean that applications for the grant of a compulsory licence are automatically accepted. The comptroller general of the Patent Office has the final say and the applicant for such a licence needs to show that he is capable of working the invention in the United Kingdom to a sufficient level. Even then, the comptroller has a general discretion and may not grant a compulsory licence if the patent holder is able to convince him that the invention will be worked to its fullest extent in the reasonably near future.

Similar conditions apply with regard to the granting of compulsory licences for registered designs although very few such licences are ever applied for since, by their nature, registered designs tend only to protect designs which are fashionable in the relatively short term and competitors are always able to choose alternative designs to manufacture and sell. A more fundamental reason lies in the fact that a patent essentially protects the inventive concept behind a new or improved product or process, and hence for potential competitors the ability to use patented technology, even if under the terms of a licence, is much more valuable than being able to copy someone else's design.

Licences of right

Another form of licence available to third parties is in respect of a patent which is endorsed 'Licence of Right', meaning that any person may apply to the patentee for a licence and cannot be refused. If the terms offered by the patentee are unacceptable to the potential licensee an application can be made for the matter to be settled by the Patent Office by means of standard licensing terms and royalty rates, which are usually at the centre of the dispute between the parties.

Licences of right arise in two ways, the first being historical in that before the Patents Act 1977 came into force the standard duration of a patent was 16 years from the date of filing, but the new Act extended this to 20 years. In order to avoid any unfairness arising between existing patent owners and those who would obtain patents under the new Act, transitional provisions were introduced whereby for all patents existing prior to 1 July 1978 which were less than 11 years old, their maximum 16-year term was extended by 4 years. However, to avoid any hardship to competitors, licences of right were made available for the final 4-year term. Thus, the last of these old Act-extended patents will expire in 1997.

Reduction of renewal cost

The second way of obtaining a licence of right is of a more permanent nature and is designed to assist owners of patents who cannot afford to pay the full annual cost of maintaining them in force. Commendably, the law allows such owners the opportunity to pay only half of the yearly renewal fee, in return for which the patent is endorsed 'Licence of Right' and anyone may apply for a licence on terms to be agreed between the parties or, in the absence of agreement, by the Patent Office. Since, as will be seen from Chapter 14, the cumulative cost of maintaining a patent in force for its full 20-year term can be quite significant, this scheme represents a useful cost-saving tool for small to medium-sized businesses, or even to large businesses who do not particularly want to monopolize an invention and would be just as happy to receive a royalty income from those wishing to work it whilst at the same time cutting down on maintenance expenses. A similar scheme is not, however, available in respect of registered designs since these are renewed at 5-year periods up to the maximum 25-year term now available and are, in any event, much cheaper to maintain in force.

Design right

It was seen from Chapter 5 that a new design right was created by the Copyright, Designs and Patents Act 1988, replacing the copyright previously enjoyed in respect of the design of any aspect of the shape or configuration (whether internal or external) of the whole or part of a functional article. The maximum duration of a design right is 15 years but can be only 10 years. Licences of right are available in respect of design rights for the final 5 years on terms again to be settled by the comptroller general of the Patent Office in the event of any dispute between the parties.

Since the law relating to the new design right has only recently been implemented there have been no instances of third parties requesting licences of right and it will be interesting to find out what happens when such applications first become possible towards the end of this century, particularly since the law has been drafted to make it almost impossible for third parties to calculate when the design right expires and therefore when the final 5-year term commences.

Trade marks

Although licensing of patents, registered designs, copyrights, design rights and know-how is generally a straightforward matter the same is not true with respect to the licensing of trade marks. It will be recalled from the previous chapter that there are unique problems associated with the buying and selling of trade marks which are caused, ultimately, by the dichotomy existing between recognizing the right of a trade mark owner to apply the trade mark to the goods or services so as to distinguish those as being exclusively associated with him, whilst at the same time permitting the sale of the trade mark, with or without the goodwill, to someone else. The same problems occur when a trade mark is to be licensed, and whilst the law allows licensing, it again imposes strict conditions upon the manner of use of the trade mark so as to minimize the risk of confusion or deception of the public when the trade mark is being used.

Control of the licensee

To avoid this risk the law requires that the trade mark owner must exercise control over the manner of use of the mark by the licensee. No particular form of control is specified, although usually this will either be quality control over the products or services on which the trade mark is being used by the licensee, or financial control where, for example, the licensor owns a majority shareholding and thus a controlling interest in the licensee. Whatever the form of the control, it must be real and continuous. If either no control exists or there has been inadequate control over the licensee's use of the trade mark to the extent that the trade or public are or have been deceived as to the nature, quality or substance of the goods or services sold under the mark, then this always constitutes a ground for invalidating the mark, if it is registered, and for the licensee to acquire exclusive rights in the mark whether or not it is registered.

A sample case

To illustrate by way of a specific example, the American owners of the famous Bostitch mark for office staplers and staples nearly lost it to a UK licensee in 1963 because although the mark had been licensed to the UK company for many years there had been little or no control over its use by the licensor. The licensee sought to invalidate the trade mark registration with the object of acquiring exclusive rights in the trade mark itself but, in a highly questionable decision, the Court held that the mark was still validly registered because a 'trade connection' had existed all along between the parties since the licensee had been using designs and know-how supplied by the licensor.

Importance of a continuing interest

Although the trade mark owner was ultimately victorious, the Bostitch case nevertheless serves as a salutary reminder that any relationship between a licensor and licensee should never be treated as anything other than 'arm's length' and appropriate safeguards employed unless the licensor owns a controlling interest in the licensee. To avoid problems of such a nature occurring, the safeguards for owners of trade marks who wish to license them are that they must maintain a continuing interest in how the marks are being used and, in particular, ensure that the quality of the goods or services on which the trade mark is being used remains constant. This requires, as a minimum, that the licensor must regularly inspect the goods or services offered under the mark, and it would also be prudent to keep records to show when the inspections were carried out and whether the required quality standards were met on each occasion. If quality standards vary then this should be rectified since otherwise use of the mark will become deceptive, in that consumers paying for a product or a service may receive in return less than they expected.

It follows that the popular misconception that trade marks can be licensed at will and, in particular, sub-licensed, has no basis whatsoever in law. To maintain exclusive ownership in a trade mark there must always be a direct connection between the owner and the end user, and the owner must exercise control over the manner of the use. The 'control' referred to earlier cannot be derogated to a third party. Hence, tax planning arrangements which establish trade mark holding companies, often offshore, and which license the use of the trade mark to others in return for royalty payments are fundamentally flawed unless the holding company is willing and able to exercise control over the manner of the use of the mark by the licensee.

Registration of licences

Trade mark licences can be registered at the Trade Marks Registry although it is not mandatory to do so. In order to qualify for registration the licence must conform to certain minimum requirements imposed by the registrar and must specifically indicate:

1. the nature of the control the owner proposes to exercise over the user (the licensee);
2. whether the licensee is to be the sole (or the exclusive) user of the mark or whether the licensor reserves the right to appoint other licensees;
3. whether the licensee is permitted to use the trade mark on all of the

goods or services covered by the registration or only on some of them, and
4. the duration, if any, of the licence or whether the licence has no fixed term.

The above information must be verified by a statutory declaration signed by the trade mark owner before a solicitor, notary public, justice of the peace, or commissioner for oaths. The registrar will then examine the application and if all appears to be in order an entry will be made in the Register formally recording the licensee as a registered user of the trade mark.

The advantage of recording a licensee as a registered user is that in order to qualify as such the terms of the licence have, necessarily, been approved by the registrar of trade marks. Whilst this does not obviate the need for continuing control by the licensor over the use of the mark, nevertheless it represents at least an official acknowledgement that the proposed manner of use is considered to be satisfactory in law.

An important additional reason for recording a licensee as a registered user arises when the trade mark owner does not itself use the mark and relies upon the use solely by the licensee. Ordinarily, this would be unacceptable since a prerequisite of the trade mark law is that a registered trade mark must be used by the proprietor. However, the law provides that registration of a licensee as a registered user enables the proprietor to assume, in law, the benefit of the use of the trade mark made by the licensee, thereby enabling the owner of the mark validly to maintain the registration.

Franchising

A franchise is a type of licence which almost always includes the right to use a trade mark, usually within a specified geographical area, which may be quite small in the case of a franchise for a fast-food outlet, or quite large where the franchise concerns a product or service which has to be sold or offered on a door-to-door basis. The primary difference between a franchise and an ordinary kind of licence lies in the fact that the giver of the franchise, the franchisor, is obligated throughout the term of the franchise to assist the recipient, the franchisee, to ensure that the franchised business is operated as efficiently and profitably as possible. For that purpose, the franchise will usually require the franchisor to provide training to the franchisee and its employees and may supply raw materials, promotional brochures, instruction manuals, uniforms and advertising. In short, the franchisee is given everything needed to set himself up in business including the related goodwill of the franchisor's trade mark. This assistance is maintained throughout the term of the franchise by the franchisor closely monitoring the quality of the goods or services offered under the franchise and other franchises granted elsewhere. In return, the franchisee usually pays an entry fee for the franchise plus a percentage of the profits earned which is, naturally enough, at a higher level than a royalty paid under a standard trade mark licence.

The risks for the franchisee

For the franchisor, the granting of a franchise is a relatively risk-free exercise provided the franchisee is willing to work hard and maintain the necessary standards to preserve the goodwill attached to the franchised business. However, for the franchisee there are risks, since a considerable initial investment in terms of time and money is usually required to get the business going, even with the assistance of the franchisor, and when the business becomes profitable it still potentially only has a limited life span for the owner of the franchise because most franchises are granted for fixed terms. Whilst a franchisor is unlikely to terminate or refuse to continue with a franchise operated by a successful franchisee, nevertheless there is still a risk that a franchisee may find that a successful business built up over several years is terminated in favour of someone else who then takes over the franchise for the same geographical area. Thus, considerable care should be exercised by any potential franchisee prior to entering into a franchise and consideration given to the possible consequences of either failing to establish a successful business after much expense and effort has been expended or, once having established the business, not being able to continue with it after the initial term of the franchise expires.

12 Valuation and taxation of intellectual property rights

In business terms a characteristic of the last 10 years or so has been the tremendous increase in the number of company mergers and acquisitions. Whilst the age of the corporate raider and leveraged buy-out may have passed its peak, nevertheless as a result there is now much more awareness of the importance of ascertaining the true value of intellectual property, as reflected in the company balance sheet. Accounting practices in the United Kingdom have experienced a revolution, moving from a position where intellectual property rights were not even mentioned on a company's balance sheet, to a position where a significant proportion of net asset value is now attributed to a company's intellectual property portfolio, particularly its trade marks.

For companies with strong brand images, such as Kodak, Coca-Cola, Cartier and Rolex, there can be no argument that their single most valuable asset is their trade mark. Without them, the companies compete for business like everyone else, having to justify their prices to the end consumer. With them, the consumer pays a premium for a product of known quality and the trade mark owner's business becomes more profitable. Industry sources in the United States have valued the MARLBORO trade mark as being worth US$40 billion worldwide.

Valuation

Interest in the correct valuation of intellectual property rights has stemmed from the desire of businesses to increase their perceived net asset value in order to increase the ability to borrow money, or increase the purchase price of the business if it is being sold or merged with another. For once, it appears that the United Kingdom has led the way in changing its accounting practices and it is a surprising fact that many businesses in other countries still do not take full advantage of the opportunities afforded by having a proper valuation of their intellectual property rights.

Since intellectual property rights are intangible it follows that they are difficult to value accurately and there is no fixed accounting method employed. On the contrary, just as with any other kind of economic theory, there are many different methodologies which may be used, depending upon the accountants' preferences and the nature of the intellectual property right. The purpose of this chapter is not to discuss all these methodologies in detail but instead to look at a few of them as they relate to the most commonly valued form of intellectual property, trade marks.

Trade marks

Market value

The most obvious and simplistic way of valuing a trade mark is to look at its market value, i.e. what the trade mark would be worth if it was offered for sale. This methodology relies upon three basic assumptions, the first being that there exists a potential buyer who would be willing to pay a fair market price for the mark. The second is that to assess what the fair market price is, it is possible to identify the price paid for similar trade marks in recent transactions. The third assumption is that market conditions are stable, which of course they never are. In most instances, the 'market value' approach is difficult to apply without, in the end, succumbing to speculation and subjectivity and it therefore cannot, in the author's view, represent anything like a scientific approach capable of facing up to close scrutiny.

Market capitalization

Another method of valuation can be termed the 'market capitalization' approach. Take, for example, a publicly listed company with shares worth £100 million and fixed assets represented by real estate and machinery of, say, £25 million. Obviously, something must be worth £75 million and it is tempting to apportion most of this to the trade marks used in the business, including the goodwill associated with them. This is not a bad start but ignores other influences such as the effect of competitive and efficient practices the company may adopt in conducting its business which make it more profitable than its competitors to the extent that shares are valued comparatively highly. Also, some businesses are naturally more profitable than others simply due to the different nature of the products or services concerned. Even so, using the market capitalization approach it is at least possible to identify the upper limit of what a trade mark is worth and to that extent this approach is a useful one.

Premium price to earnings

Another method again assumes that comparisons can be made with similar kinds of businesses and is the 'premium price to earnings' method. In essence, this method states that if a similar business exists without any trade marks (almost impossible) and can be purchased for X, then a corresponding business which includes recognized trade marks and has a higher price to earnings ratio necessarily must attribute the difference to the value of the trade marks. Again, this ignores other factors which can influence the end result and necessarily relies upon there being a conveniently available business of a similar kind and size, recently sold, without any trade marks but still providing maintainable earnings in stable market conditions.

Replacement cost

Another method which has some attraction is called the 'replacement cost' method, being simply the summation of the total of what it would cost if the existing trade mark were abandoned and a new one was chosen and promoted to the extent that it achieves the same level of recognition and popularity to consumers. In short, this system states that if a business had to stop using its trade mark tomorrow, how much would it cost to retrieve its business using another trade mark? Again, however, it will be appreciated that any judgements based upon this methodology are necessarily highly subjective and are therefore difficult to justify in scientific terms.

Relief from royalty

All these methods of valuing trade marks suffer from fairly fundamental flaws but there is another which is not quite so bad, although none is perfect. This is the 'relief from royalty' approach and is based, ultimately, on the realization that modern business practices often include licensing and franchising of trade marks throughout a broad spectrum of business activities. It is therefore relatively easy to determine what the average royalty rate is for using well-known trade marks in particular industries. In the clothing industry, depending upon the trade mark in question, reasonably famous trade marks can be licensed for 5 or 10 per cent of the net sales value of the products. Therefore, a garment manufacturer selling garments under a particular trade mark can assume that if he did not own the trade mark he would have to pay royalties to a third party at a fixed rate. Using this method, the value of the trade mark is clearly the cumulative cost of the royalties, after tax, but capitalized using a discount rate of, say, 25 per cent, estimating the future turnover, allowing for the effect of profits tax, and assuming that there will be no material changes in the market or taking account of any expected changes.

Using this method it is possible to calculate what the trade mark is worth to the trade mark owner if it were to be exclusively licensed on 'arm's length' terms and hence it is a reasonable method for valuing trade marks for any business for the purposes of incorporating such a valuation in the balance sheet.

Conclusion

These valuation techniques are mentioned briefly simply to illustrate the various kinds of considerations which may apply but, as explained, there is no general agreement as to which is the most accurate and there is always a risk that a trade mark may be valued incorrectly, sometimes by a very wide margin. If the valuation is simply for company audit purposes this may not be too problematic but if it is being made in order to form the basis of the sale of a trade mark considerable caution should be exercised by the intended purchaser. Similarly, financial institutions being asked to take security interests in trade marks or other forms of intellectual property need to exercise the greatest caution since it is clear that, whatever methodology is used, it is relatively easy to overinflate the value by using optimistic assumptions. Expert advice from a chartered accountant should always be sought, preferably from one who has experience in dealing with this very special area of accountancy.

Taxation aspects

Because intellectual property rights have traditionally been given only a nominal value, often simply the cost of obtaining a patent or registering a trade mark, taxation aspects have until recently been largely ignored. However, as true market valuations have increasingly been sought, so has the importance of tax considerations grown. With them have come changes in UK tax law which is now extremely complex and is only summarized briefly in this chapter.

Stamp duty

The simplest form of tax is popularly called stamp duty which is an *ad valorem* tax imposed on most kinds of property transfers including real estate when the sale price is above a certain threshold – presently £60,000. Stamp duty is payable by the purchaser, currently at the rate of 1 per cent of the purchase price, although a deduction can be claimed if the purchase of intellectual property qualifies as a capital expense for the business. The duty only becomes payable if the document transferring the intellectual property (which may include foreign rights) is executed in the United Kingdom, or if the intellectual property being transferred exists in the United Kingdom. A transfer of a property is also deemed to have occurred in respect of the granting of an exclusive licence and hence also attracts stamp duty if the value of the licence exceeds the threshold level.

If foreign intellectual property rights are being transferred or exclusively licensed at the same time, it is therefore usual practice first, to sign the documents outside the United Kingdom and keep them there and, second, to separate the transfer into two parts, one set of documentation relating solely to the UK intellectual property rights and the other dealing with the foreign rights. Doing this ensures that the minimum amount of stamp duty is payable on the transaction.

Time limit

A document transferring an intellectual property right or granting an exclusive licence under one must be presented for assessment of stamp duty within 30 days of its execution or, if executed outside the United Kingdom, within 30 days of first having been received there. If the document is not presented for assessment until later, then a fine for late payment is imposed, the fine increasing with time. If the transfer document is not presented at all, it cannot be used in Court to show that a transfer of the intellectual property right has occurred or that an exclusive licence has been granted, as the case may be. Since the primary function of any intellectual property right is to try to prevent others from exploiting it, if necessary by enforcing rights in the Courts, it therefore follows that failure to pay stamp duty can have very serious consequences when infringement occurs.

Incorrect valuation

Historically, owners of intellectual property rights have been tempted to value them at nominal consideration for the purposes of avoiding undue exposure to stamp duty, but nowadays an obviously undervalued transfer will usually be questioned by the Inland Revenue who may then make their own assessment as to what the intellectual property is worth.

If, however, the assignment or exclusive licence is below the threshold level of £60,000 it is not necessary to present the document for assessment at all, provided it contains what is called a 'certificate of value' clause confirming that the aggregate value of the transaction on its own or as part of a series of transactions does not exceed £60,000.

VAT

Value added tax is chargeable on intellectual property rights just as if they were any other form of property except that their provision is regarded as the supply of a service. This means that a person granting a licence under an intellectual property right in return for a royalty, or selling the right in return for a lump sum payment must, if he is VAT registered (or should be), withhold VAT at the standard rate. However, if the supply of the intellectual property rights is outside the United Kingdom then, generally speaking, no VAT is payable. Even so, the position, particularly with regard to the supply of services within other member states of the EEC, can be quite complex and will depend whether the recipient of the right receives it in a business capacity or not.

Other taxes payable

Liability to income tax, capital gains tax and corporation tax depends upon the nature of the transaction (in particular whether money received from the transaction is to be taken as a trading receipt or a capital gain) and the nature of the intellectual property rights, how they have arisen, and how the money is being earned. A patent is treated differently to other forms of intellectual property and a lump sum received in respect of the sale of the patent is regarded as a capital gain. For the purchaser of the patent an allowance can therefore be claimed in respect of the money spent if it has been purchased for use in the production of business profits in the United Kingdom. If only part of the patent rights have been purchased for use in the UK, then that part which can be reasonably attributed to the production of profits in the UK is tax-deductible.

The taxation of the sale proceeds of trade marks, registered designs and design rights depends on a variety of factors such as residence, place of incorporation, what the receipt is for and whether it is of an income or capital nature; and what expenditures are deductible, such as expenditures relating to the creation and maintenance of the trade mark, registered design or design right. Even so, as a general rule, income received from the disposal of an intellectual property right either through direct sale or by the grant of an exclusive licence will be regarded as capital in nature, whereas royalties received by the grant of a non-exclusive licence to one or more parties will be regarded as being in the nature of an income and thus subject to income tax. The situation is, however, extremely complex and expert advice should be sought whenever large sums of money are involved such as with an outright sale, or cumulatively such as in respect of repayment by instalments of capital outlay, or ongoing payment of royalties for intellectual property rights which are licensed.

13 Costs

It has been a continuing theme of this book that the complex requirements of intellectual property make it necessary to rely to a large extent on professional help. To devote a complete chapter to the subject of costs is simply a reflection of this. By now, it is hoped that the reader will have acquired a basic understanding of a variety of essential aspects of intellectual property and from which it should be clear that acquiring such rights can sometimes be as expensive as enforcing them through the Courts.

The use of agents

Most patents, registered designs and registered trade marks are obtained using the services of patent agents and trade mark agents whose hourly charge-out rates often equal or even exceed those of other professional advisers such as solicitors and accountants. This is not surprising since their professional qualifications are every bit as difficult to acquire, some would say more so. It should not be forgotten that these people are in business too and it is not their role to advise clients on whether, for example, too much money is being spent on acquiring or enforcing any particular intellectual property right. That is a commercial decision usually made by the manager of the business, but often made too late or without any real appreciation as to how costs can rapidly accumulate to an alarmingly high level. Problems with cost overruns usually stem from an initial desire to seek as much protection as is available, particularly when patent, design or trade mark rights are sought overseas.

Basic costs

Acquiring intellectual property rights in the United Kingdom is relatively inexpensive and not beyond the means of most businesses. The costs primarily arise in two ways, the first being the relatively modest official fees charged by the government, and the second being the much higher professional fees charged by the firms of patent or trade mark agents. However, once a patent, registered design or registered trade mark is applied for in another country this almost inevitably has to be with the assistance of a foreign firm of patent or trade mark agents who also charge for their services, thus effectively adding an extra layer of professional charges. There is little that can be done to avoid this since if, for example, patent applications are being filed in a number of countries then in each a patent agent must be employed to deal with the formalities and any objections raised by the patent office during the prosecution of the application. The firm of patent agents used in the United Kingdom will normally need to coordinate what is happening elsewhere to ensure consistency of approach, thus avoiding a situation arising whereby a relatively narrow patent is obtained in one country as compared to another.

Renewals

The same is even true in respect of renewal of patents, designs and trade marks even if renewal is handled by a specialist agency. In most instances, payment of the renewal fee can only be made in any particular country by a local firm of patent or trade mark agents and thus even the payment of a renewal fee to maintain an intellectual property right in force outside the United Kingdom will still usually involve the payment of an official fee, foreign agents' charges and, of course, the fees charged by the renewal agency itself.

The importance of sufficient protection

For those businesses which are aware of the cumulative costs of obtaining and maintaining intellectual property rights it is often tempting to spend the absolute minimum on protecting their rights at home or abroad, which is just as big a mistake as spending too much and then finding that the business cannot operate profitably because too much time, effort and expenditure is being used up to the exclusion of running the business. Very large companies can usually absorb the costs of obtaining fairly comprehensive protection for their intellectual property rights effectively worldwide, but very few small to medium-sized businesses can. Those businesses seeking 100 per cent protection are seeking the impossible, whereas those businesses which fail to protect themselves adequately in their major markets will often find it difficult to compete effectively.

To illustrate, it is useful to look at the numbers of European (EPC) patent applications filed by UK companies as compared with those from countries with broadly similar economies. In 1991 British companies filed a total of 2902 such patent applications at either the UK Patent Office or at the European Patent Office in Munich. In contrast, Germany filed 10 467 applications, France filed 4537 and, not surprisingly, Japan filed no less than 12 272. The United States led the way with 14 991 applications filed.

Britain has the unfortunate reputation of being good at inventing but bad at exploiting, which is clearly reflected in these figures. It is impossible fully to exploit an invention if insufficient patent protection is sought because competitors are free to copy the invention in countries where there are no patents. On the other hand, only a relatively small percentage of all patents ever prove to be commercially valuable and worth the effort and expense in obtaining them. This does not mean that the prudent businessman should simply ignore patenting altogether, but rather that patent filing programmes should be reviewed at regular intervals to assess viability given the commercial success or otherwise of a newly invented product or process for which patent protection is being sought. As mentioned previously, it often takes two to four years to obtain a patent and the initial enthusiasm for filing applications in a large number of countries may later prove to be unfounded, in which case the filing programme can be pruned accordingly, or even scrapped altogether so that the money saved can be better utilized elsewhere in the business.

This chapter only deals with the costs of acquiring and maintaining patents, registered designs and trade marks since copyright, design rights and know-how are, once created, already fully exploitable and require no significant further action on the part of the owner. The specific costs quoted will necessarily rapidly become out of date but should nevertheless still provide a useful guide provided allowances are made for inflation.

Patenting costs

Patents are by far the most expensive rights to acquire and they are also the most unpredictable in terms of costs. A relatively simple invention does not necessarily translate into a relatively inexpensive patenting procedure, just as a technically difficult invention may not necessarily turn out to cost more. The factors which influence the overall cost are as follows:

- The subject matter of the invention.
- The nature and quantity of objections raised by the Patent Office during the application procedure.
- The competence of the patent agent.
- The amount of effort expended by the applicant.

The subject matter of the application

Generally speaking, the subject matter of the invention primarily affects the initial costs of the patent application procedure. A relatively simple invention is relatively simple for a patent agent to describe and therefore the time taken to prepare the patent specification is proportionately less than for a technically complex invention.

As will be seen from Appendix 1, the patent specification almost always includes a preamble portion describing the background technical art to which the invention belongs, a brief description of what the invention is followed by a detailed description with reference to the drawings, followed finally by the most important and difficult part to draft, the patent claims themselves. The official filing fees at the Patent Office are the same whether the patent specification is 10 or a 100 pages long. The same is not true of the patent agent's charges, which are purely based upon the amount of time spent in preparing the document. For this reason, it is never possible to give an accurate estimate of how much it will cost to prepare and file a patent application although it should be possible to obtain a ballpark figure from the patent agent after an initial review of the invention has been made. The initial review will, if billed separately, probably only cost one or two hundred pounds whereafter the patent agent should be in a position to estimate how long it will take and hence how much it will cost to prepare a full patent specification including the necessary drawings. As a guide, a patent specification similar to that shown in Appendix 1 would cost approximately £1,500–2,000 to prepare and file at the Patent Office.

Particularly for inventions which are technically complex, significant cost savings can be made if the patent agent is provided with a clear and comprehensive description of the invention by the inventor in a written report not unlike the patent specification itself outlining the following:

- The area of technology to which the invention relates, giving specific examples of conventional existing technology and how it works.
- The technical problems which the invention seeks to overcome.
- What the invention is and how it overcomes these problems.
- What advantages the invention has over the known prior art.

With this basic information, which should include drawings, flowcharts, prototype models or any other visual data which assists in a rapid understanding of how the invention works, the patent agent's job is made much easier and less time has to be spent on preparing the patent specification and claims. This directly translates into cost savings for the owner of the invention which can be significant, bearing in mind that many firms of patent agents charge out their time at between £150 and £250 per hour, depending upon where they are located. In any event, it is wrong to assume that a patent agent knows everything there is to know in whatever area of technology he specializes. The more information a patent agent receives from an inventor the more accurate and comprehensive is the resulting patent specification. Patent agents actually prefer receiving as much information as possible from the inventor in order to lessen the risk of making a mistake which may not be obvious to the inventor at the time but may be capable of being exploited by an infringer once the patent has been issued.

During the application procedure

The second factor affecting the cost of obtaining a patent is what happens during the application procedure which, in turn, depends upon the quality of the invention and what prior art the Patent Office staff locate during their searches. Some inventions are clearly new but may still be considered by the Patent Office as being obvious over the known prior art, thus leading to a rejection requiring the patent agent to try to overcome it by submitting extensive written arguments in the hope of persuading the examiner otherwise. Even if no fundamental objections are raised against the patentability of an invention, nevertheless one or several items of prior art are usually located by the Patent Office, which are mostly previously published patent specifications relating to the same area of technology. If 10 patent specifications are cited by the examiner, each one has to be reviewed by the patent agent and points of difference and similarity noted. When this happens, it is often the case that the cost of assessing the prior art, amending the patent claims and formulating arguments in reply to the examiner will exceed even the cost of preparing and filing the patent specification. Even so, costs can be saved by using a little common sense by the inventor carrying out an initial review of any cited prior art himself and highlighting those which appear to be the closest to the invention. However, if an invention is an important one it may still be necessary to have the patent agent review all the prior art documents to ensure that nothing is missed which could either affect the chances of obtaining a patent or the validity of a subsequently granted patent. A throw-away sentence tucked away in an obscure part of an otherwise apparently irrelevant patent specification can sometimes prove to be the undoing of a granted patent or require it to be amended in order to preserve validity.

The applicant's involvement

The amount of effort expended by the owner of a patent application will also affect the total cost. Money can be saved by assisting the patent agent as much as possible but, equally, money can be lost by requiring the agent to carry on with the application procedure by making repeated and lengthy submissions to the Patent Office, even when it is clear that there is little chance of obtaining worthwhile patent protection for the invention. Conscious efforts need to be made to review at regular intervals the benefits of continuing with the application procedure as compared to the costs involved.

Except for inventions which are completely anticipated by the prior art, it is almost always possible to obtain a patent by narrowing down the claims to such a level that they are distinguished from the prior art. However, the narrower a claim is the easier it is for a competitor to avoid infringement by making minor changes to the product or process and a point is reached when the potential benefits of obtaining a patent are outweighed by the cost and effort involved. Ideally, before that point is reached a decision should have been made as to whether to continue with the application or abandon it by asking a simple question, 'Is worthwhile patent protection available for the invention?'. The answer to this will usually require some input from the patent agent, who should be able to identify the general scope of the claims which may be available for the invention and how easily it would be for competitors to avoid infringing them whilst still benefiting from the advantages afforded by the invention over the prior art.

Conclusion

It will be seen from the foregoing that it is not possible to predict accurately, even for budgetary purposes, the likely expenses involved in obtaining a patent, although experience suggests that as a general rule if the cost of filing a patent application is multiplied by three then in many instances this will represent the total cost involved. Of this, one-third can be apportioned to the patent agent's charges in preparing and filing the application and payment of the official fees. One-third can be attributed to a variety of formalities which have to be attended to during the prosecution process including the filing of various forms and payment of official fees such as for the preliminary examination and search and the fee for requesting substantive examination. The final third will represent the patent agent's professional time in dealing with objections raised during the examination process up to grant or refusal of the patent. Using this scheme and assuming that the invention is of a fairly simple nature such as is illustrated in Appendix 1, it is possible to make reasonable assumptions as to what costs will be incurred during the various stages of a UK patent application, as shown in Table 13.1.

It must be remembered that Table 13.1 is based upon a variety of assumptions and is of course limited solely to the United Kingdom.

Table 13.1 Estimated cost for obtaining a UK patent for an invention which can be described in a 3000-word patent specification (see Appendix 1).

Action required	When required	Estimated cost
Preparation and filing of patent specification and drawings	(Filing date)	£1,000–2,000
Filing request for preliminary examination and search	Within 12 months of filing date	£250
Filing statement of inventorship	Within 16 months of filing date	£40
Publication of patent application by Patent Office	18 months after filing date	Nil (usually part of fee for search request)
Requesting substantive examination	Within 6 months of publication	£275
Receiving, considering and replying to examiner's first report	Within 6 months of receiving report	£50–1,000 (according to complexity)
Dealing with each subsequent examination report	Within 4 months of receiving report	£50
Grant of patent	Within 4½ years from filing date	£100

Where national patent rights are being sought elsewhere the applicant should expect to pay at least the same because although the cost of preparing the patent specification will already have been met, this is counterbalanced by the cost of the additional patent agency services in those countries where corresponding patent applications have been filed. Additionally, many countries require translations of English language patent specifications into their own language, the costs for which can be significant. Another influencing factor is that the cost of such legal services varies from country to country and are significantly higher in some, such as the United States and Japan, than in others, particularly the less developed countries.

Costs can be reduced or delayed by taking advantage of either the European Patent Convention or the Patent Cooperation Treaty (discussed in Chapter 2), but even then it will be obvious that the cumulative cost of seeking patent protection in, say, Europe, North America and Japan is still significant and needs to be constantly monitored as the applications progress to ensure that such costs do not get out of hand or are being incurred unnecessarily.

Once a patent is granted, renewal fees must be paid which, for most countries of the world which issue patents, are payable on a yearly basis. The only notable exception is the United States, which requires renewal fees at, respectively, 3-and-a-half, 7-and-a-half and 11-and-a-half years from the date of grant. As mentioned previously, the renewal fee cannot be taken in isolation since professional charges will also be incurred by the firm actually paying the fee in each country.

Table 13.2 Renewal fees for UK effective patents

Year	Agency costs	Official fee	Total
5th	£40	£110	£150
6th	£40	£120	£160
7th	£40	£130	£170
8th	£40	£140	£180
9th	£40	£150	£190
10th	£40	£170	£210
11th	£40	£190	£230
12th	£40	£210	£250
13th	£40	£230	£270
14th	£40	£260	£300
15th	£40	£280	£320
16th	£40	£310	£350
17th	£40	£340	£380
18th	£40	£370	£410
19th	£40	£410	£450
20th	£40	£450	£490

In the United Kingdom, renewal fees are required from the end of the fourth year up to the twentieth year, as can be seen from Table 13.2.

For patents which have been effectively extended up to the maximum of 25 years permissible by the grant of a Supplementary Protection Certificate (see Chapter 2), usually patents relating to drugs, yearly renewal fees are payable, in advance, for the final five years. Currently, these fees amount in total to £3,900, to which should be added the filing fee for obtaining a SPC of £250 plus, of course, the patent agent's fees of approximately £150.

As can be seen, the renewal fees are not significant when taken in isolation but for a company owning several patents in a large number of countries the situation is rather different. Accordingly, it is unwise to issue instructions for the automatic payment of a renewal fee whenever it becomes due for all but the most important inventions since the cost of maintaining a patent generally increases yearly in most countries, whereas it is often the case that the worth of a patent decreases as a result of new technology coming along replacing the old. For these reasons it is prudent to carry out yearly reviews of the patent portfolio, abandoning as necessary those patents no longer useful to the business and only renewing those which are worth while.

Registered design costs

The cost of obtaining a registered design is almost insignificant in comparison to that for a patent. The reason is that there is little technical input involved and the examination is much less strict, sometimes appearing even cursory. This is not always the case elsewhere and,

Table 13.3 Estimated cost for obtaining and maintaining a registered design

Action required	Estimated cost
Preparing and filing the application, including preparing drawings or photographs of the design	£400
Receiving, considering and replying to each examination report	£50–200 (often an application proceeds to registration without an examination report issuing)
Renewal 5 years after filing and then at 5-year intervals	1st period £200 2nd period £275

notably, the United States carries out a very thorough examination which includes a comprehensive search for prior art designs, before issuing its equivalent to a UK registered design, a US design patent.

Similarly, renewal fees are commensurately lower than for patents and for a UK registered design they are only required at five-year intervals. Table 13.3 summarizes the costs involved in obtaining and maintaining a registered design and similar charges can be anticipated in most other countries where such design protection is available.

Trade mark registration costs

There can be an enormous disparity in the cost of registering one mark as compared to another and this is almost always due to the nature of the mark itself. It will be recalled from Chapter 3 that some trade marks are extremely easy to register because they automatically qualify for registration, particularly those marks which are inherently distinctive and do not suggest the character or quality of the goods or services in question, or their geographical origin. At the other end of the scale are those marks which are fundamentally difficult to register and therefore can only be registered with a great deal of effort and hence expense. The effort is usually in the form of providing evidence that the mark has acquired distinctiveness through many years use in the United Kingdom, coupled with articulate and extensive arguments submitted by the trade mark agent used to register the mark. Often, this work will include detailed reviews of the case law in respect of marks of a similar nature which have either been refused or accepted for registration in the past and even market survey evidence is sometimes required in order to show that a mark should be registered because it has become distinctive through use.

Despite this, since trade marks do not have a limited life span as do patents and registered designs and can be extremely valuable to a business, as was seen in the previous chapter, there really is no choice for a business but to register its trade marks, assuming registration is

Table 13.4 Estimated cost for registering and maintaining a trade mark in one class of goods or services

Action required	Estimated cost
Preparing and filing application	£400
Receiving, considering and replying to each examination report	£50 upwards (according to complexity)
Acceptance of advertisement in *Trade Marks Journal* and registration mark	£100
Renewal 7 years after filing original application and then at 14-year intervals	£350

possible at all. This does not mean that all trade marks used in the business should necessarily be registered, since there is little point in spending money on marks which are used for seasonal promotions or are of relatively short-term duration. For those trade marks which are considered long-term the overall cost of registration, even for marks which are difficult to register, is still negligible compared to the value of the mark. To illustrate, if the Eastman Kodak Company had not registered its mark KODAK up to now but had just decided to do so, the few thousand pounds it would spend on the exercise would represent an insignificant proportion of the value of the mark. This does not mean that registration is essential since common law rights can often be relied upon, but registration is a neat and effective way of establishing statutory legal rights and also provides other benefits to the trade mark owner which are not available under the common law.

Assuming a mark qualifies for registration and there are no identical or similar third-party marks already on the Register for the same or similar goods or services then Table 13.4 illustrates the anticipated costs involved in a straightforward case for registering one mark in one class and paying renewal fees to keep the mark in force. It should, however, be borne in mind that the United Kingdom adopts a system of registration on a class-by-class basis. More often than not a trade mark is being used on goods or services falling in several classes so that several separate registrations may have to be obtained and maintained in order fully to protect the mark. Similar considerations apply in many other countries, although most European countries permit the filing of one application covering several classes of goods or services but charge a slightly higher fee for each additional class after the first.

Conclusion

There are other costs which should be considered, apart from those for obtaining and maintaining patents, registered designs and registered trade marks. These arise in a variety of circumstances, such as the following:

- When an intellectual property right is sold there is the cost of preparing the assignment document itself, recording the transfer of ownership and paying stamp duty and/or VAT if applicable.
- If the owner is a company which changes its name or address, this should be officially recorded although the cost is relatively insignificant.
- In the case of trade marks, if a licensee is appointed an application should be made to the Trade Marks Registry to record the licensee as a registered user of the mark for the reasons outlined in Chapter 11.
- Before adopting a new trade mark, manufacturing and selling a new product or using a new process, it is prudent to carry out clearance searches beforehand, as was discussed in Chapter 9. Trade mark and design searches can usually be undertaken for a few hundred pounds in most countries but a reasonably comprehensive prior art search relating to a new area of technology which may be the subject of existing patents is likely to cost at least £1,000 to £1,500 and could be considerably more if the subject matter is particularly complex and there is a large amount of prior art to review.
- If the business subscribes to a watching service in order to alert it to competitors seeking to patent similar technology or register similar trade marks there will be an annual charge for the service and an additional charge for all documents supplied.

This list of situations which can give rise to additional charges illustrates how easy it is to underestimate the overall cost of acquiring and maintaining intellectual property rights.

Finally, this chapter on costs would not be complete without a reminder to the reader of the tax deductibility of some of these costs, particularly those which are directly necessary for the production of business profits.

14 Keeping intellectual property rights in force

Intellectual property rights are kept in force in a variety of ways, depending upon the nature of the right concerned. Know-how, or confidential information as it is often called, is retained as a property right simply by keeping it secret, or at least obliging persons licensed to use the know-how to keep it secret. As soon as the know-how enters the public domain, whether accidentally or as a result of a breach on the part of a licensee, the right disappears, although if there has been unauthorized disclosure then action can be taken in the Court to seek appropriate remedies.

Copyright and design right

Copyright is a right which arises automatically and is of a fixed duration, generally being 50 years after the death of the author of the copyright work or, if the copyright is in respect of sound recordings, films, broadcasts and cable programmes, 50 years from the end of the first year in which the copyright work was made public, such as by the screening of a film if the subject of the copyright is a film. Accordingly, once a copyright is established it costs nothing to maintain and cannot be extinguished until its full term expires, although this does not mean that the copyright owner would necessarily always wish to enforce the copyright against third parties who may wish to use the copyright work for themselves.

The only exception to this concerns copyright in the literary work *Peter Pan* by J. M. Barrie which, as mentioned in Chapter 5, has been treated as a special case by the Copyright, Designs and Patents Act 1988 and the copyright therein has been extended in perpetuity in order to provide a continuing source of income for the Hospital for Sick Children, Great Ormond Street, even though the original copyright in the work expired on 31 December 1987. Whilst the motives behind this special exception are commendable, it is not clear how reciprocal arrangements for protecting copyright with other countries are affected where, due to the expiration of the normal term of the copyright, persons in other countries including in the EEC are freely entitled to copy the work and make adaptations of it as desired. Since the rights in the copyright work have already been exhausted in other EEC member states, it may well be that an adaptation of the work printed by a company in another member state but sold throughout the whole of the EEC including the United Kingdom would not attract royalty, or the copyright could not be enforced.

The new design right has a much shorter term than copyright, being hypothetically anywhere between 10 and 15 years in duration and, again, no fees are required to keep a design right in force.

In contrast, the other three forms of monopolistic intellectual property rights discussed in this book, patents, registered designs and trade marks all require positive action on the part of the owner otherwise the property right will expire in a relatively short period.

Patents

Patents are kept in force for their usual maximum term of 20 years by payment of yearly renewal fees from the end of the fourth year onwards. As was seen from the previous chapter relating to costs, the renewal fees increase on a sliding scale, being relatively modest at first but increasing by about 350 per cent for the twentieth and final year. Even the owners of Supplementary Protection Certificates for pharmaceutical drugs, still have to pay (in advance) yearly renewal fees which increase up to the maximum term possible of five years. The object of this sliding-scale policy appears to be to discourage parties from needlessly maintaining a patent in force for its full term so that, in practice, only the most valuable inventions continue to be protected up to their full term. Another stated objective for the scale is that by keeping costs relatively low in the initial years, more money is then made available for exploitation of the invention by the patentee. In reality, however, it is questionable if this object is really achieved since the exploitation of an invention necessarily costs far more than the renewal fees for maintaining a patent in force.

Late payment of renewal fees

If a renewal fee is not paid on time there is a general six-month grace period for paying the fee, although a fine is imposed which increases towards the end of this six-month period. Late payment of a renewal fee within the maximum six-month period does not affect the enforceability of the patent in any way, and any act by a third party which would normally infringe the patent still does so provided the fee is paid within the six months.

However, it sometimes happens that a renewal fee which is intended by the patentee to be paid is not and the patentee does not find out about this until after the six-month period allowed for late payment. At such a point in time the patent has actually lapsed although in certain circumstances the patentee can have the patent restored if an application is made to the controller general of the Patent Office within 19 months from the date on which the original renewal fee became due, but only if the proprietor of the patent took reasonable care to ensure that the payment was to be made, even though it was not. What constitutes, 'reasonable care' is for the comptroller to decide and an application for restoration of a lapsed patent must include a statutory declaration explaining precisely what happened and, most importantly, demonstrating that the patentee exercised reasonable care to ensure that the patent was renewed on time. This requirement of reasonable care will generally mean in practice entrusting the renewal to a firm of patent agents used to obtain the patent, or to one of several specialist renewal agencies which have been set up around the world to deal with these tasks.

Although it is possible to restore a patent which has lapsed, there clearly have to be safeguards to protect competitors who may have in the intervening period, in good faith, begun using the invention. It would be unfair to prevent such parties from continuing to use the invention since to do so would, effectively, make them pay for the patentee's error. The law solves this problem for persons who in good faith carried out acts which would otherwise have constituted an infringement of the patent if it had not expired, or had made in good faith serious and effective preparations to do so. Such persons are entitled to carry on, even if the patent is subsequently restored. However, this right to carry on 'infringing' the patent without the patentee being able to do anything about it does not extend to the granting of sub-licences to other persons and is therefore limited to only those persons who have been directly prejudiced by the restoration of the patent.

The consequences of failing to renew a valuable patent on time can therefore be quite serious and, always, more costly than if the renewal fee had been paid on time. Prior to the coming into force of the 1988 Act, the requirements to renew on time were even more stringent and, often due to simple clerical errors being made, many important patents were lost through failure to pay the renewal fee within the six-month statutory grace period.

Conclusion

Because renewal fees have to be paid on a regular basis over a period lasting many years, it is not safe for any business to assume that simply marking an entry in a diary every year is sufficient to avoid mistakes occurring. Personnel changes inevitably occur, as do business mergers and acquisitions, all of which tend to give rise to circumstances where there is potential for someone to forget and a mistake to occur. For this reason, the vast majority of patents, registered designs and trade marks, are renewed not by the owners but by either the patent or trade mark agents originally used to obtain the right, or by means of specialist computerized renewal agencies.

Registered designs

Unlike patents, registered designs only have to be renewed at five-year intervals but there are similar saving provisions just in case a mistake is made and the renewal fee is not paid on time. The owner of the registered design has a statutory right to pay the renewal fee during the six months immediately after the renewal fee became due, again with a fine for late payment which increases towards the end of the six-month period. As with patents, there is also a 19 month maximum within which restoration of a lapsed registered design can be applied for and, again, any such application must demonstrate that the proprietor exercised reasonable care to ensure that the fee was paid. Similarly, if restoration is allowed the same protective measures are employed to ensure that third parties who have commenced or prepared for commencement of acts which otherwise would have infringed the design had it been in force do not suffer as a result of the failure by the owner to pay the renewal fee on time.

It will be apparent that the requirement to pay renewal fees every five years in order to maintain registered designs in force really makes it even more necessary for owners to place the onus of reminding them when a renewal fee is due in the hands of others.

Trade marks

Maintaining trade marks in force is even more problematic than patents and registered designs for two reasons. The first is that the renewal fees are generally payable at much longer intervals, being originally 7 years from the date of application and thereafter at 14-year intervals. The second reason stems from earlier references in this book to various ways in which trade mark rights can become lost or unenforceable through lack of use or misuse.

The easy part is to pay the renewal fee on time using, once again, a renewal agency or the firm of patent or trade mark agents used to obtain the registration. Because of the relatively long periods between each renewal, it is also prudent to consider at the time when renewal is required if the trade mark is still relevant to the business and in particular whether it still adequately protects all the goods or services currently traded in by the company.

Renewal also affords an opportunity to consider whether greater protection can be obtained by refiling an application to register the same trade mark if the original registration was only accepted in Part B of the Register, or was subject to disclaimer of exclusive rights to part of the mark. This is because it is usually the case that if a mark has been used for at least five years to a reasonably substantial level then it is likely to have acquired a sufficient level of distinctiveness qualifying it for registration in Part A of the Register, even if the original registration may only have been obtained in Part B due to a lack of prior use or a lack of sufficient prior use. The time for renewal also provides an opportunity to update the records of the Trade Marks Registry if the proprietor has either changed its name or address.

Other ways of preserving validity

Since there is no fixed limit on the number of times that a trade mark may be renewed it therefore follows that a valid trade mark registration can last forever provided the mark is continually used and, just as importantly, provided it is continually being used properly. That a trade mark should be used in order to preserve its validity is obviously reasonable and the United Kingdom is quite generous in this respect in allowing periods of non-use for up to five years before a trade mark registration becomes vulnerable to cancellation by an interested third party. However, a registered mark may also become vulnerable for a variety of other reasons, one being where it is being licensed to another party but no control is exercised over the use of the mark. As was discussed in detail in Chapter 11, it is a requirement of the trade mark law that the trade mark owner must exercise continuous control over the activities of any licensee.

Marks which become generic terms

Another way in which a trade mark registration can become effectively invalid is if the mark is allowed to become the generic description of a product or services. Whilst HOOVER is still a registered trade mark in the United Kingdom, nevertheless it is an unfortunate fact that many people refer to vacuum cleaners as 'hoovers' and thus they are using the trade mark in a descriptive sense. Trade mark owners therefore need to be constantly vigilant to ensure that their marks are not being used descriptively, particularly if the trade mark is used on a unique type of product where there is a natural tendency of the trade and public to then refer to the product solely by the name or trade mark of the manufacturer. An example is the very popular flying disc which is sold under the registered trade mark FRISBEE. All such discs are now commonly referred to as frisbees by children and adults alike irrespective of their source.

Another example is NYLON which was a trade mark of Dupont derived for its newly invented fibre from the initial letters of New York and the first three letters of London. Nowadays, NYLON is an entirely generic term and therefore unprotectable, although the curious thing is that Dupont purposely allowed it to become a generic term in what was probably a trade-off at the time designed to ensure maximum exposure of the newly invented product which was, in any case, protected by patents owned by Dupont.

Although trade marks can easily become generic by using them as descriptive terms, they can just as easily be prevented from becoming generic by using a little common sense. To illustrate, there is a world of difference between these two slogans:

Wear Levis

Wear LEVI jeans

In the first instance, the trade mark LEVI is being used in substitution for the description of the goods, i.e. jeans, whereas in the second instance the trade mark is being used in conjunction with the description of the goods. The first risks eventual loss of exclusivity in the mark if the general trade or public, or at least a sufficiently large cross-section, come to refer to jeans as Levis. The second, proper, manner of use ensures that this can never happen and maintains the validity of the registration of the LEVI trade mark forever.

For the business manager, the golden rule for ensuring that the mark does not become descriptive and thus generic, is to identify it as a trade mark, whether or not it is a registered trade mark by always ensuring that it is used in conjunction with, rather than in substitution for, a descriptive term for the product or services. Using a mark in capital letters or in a different typeface to other words used on the product packaging or advertising also helps to indicate that it is a trade mark rather than a descriptive term available for all to use.

Conclusion

Finally, a brief mention of the situation outside the United Kingdom. In this country, patents, registered designs and trade marks are maintained in a fairly flexible manner, often forgiving of mistakes. However, in many other countries a missed deadline constitutes the loss of the right and since, above all, it is essential to keep intellectual property rights in force if they are important to a business, then it follows that great care needs to be exercised to ensure that mistakes are kept to a minimum.

The loss of an important trade mark registration in a country which does not recognize rights accruing through past use under common law principles as exist in the United Kingdom can be truly disastrous if another party has already applied to register the same or a similar mark. In those circumstances any fresh application to re-register the lost mark is likely to fail. Equally, the loss of an important patent or registered design protecting the owner from competition will, if it is important enough, soon come to the attention of competitors who are then able to compete freely. Accordingly, for those persons engaged in export businesses, where, inevitably, some form or other of intellectual property is being used, adequate steps must be taken to ensure that renewal fees are paid on time.

15 European aspects

Despite the relatively rough ride that the Maastricht Treaty has received from many Europeans, nevertheless the future direction of Europe seems clear, with monetary and political union following on the heels of the Common Market, even if somewhat reluctantly. The formation of a single unified market necessarily requires a unified set of rules and laws so that everyone is treated equally. As regards trade itself, the overriding principle is that there must be no physical or legal barriers for the free movement of goods within the Community itself. The only notable exception to this principle concerns intellectual property, except that all member states will eventually be required to harmonize their laws in terms of what rights are granted, how they are granted and how they may be enforced.

Although UK intellectual property law has changed considerably over the last 10 or 15 years, there are nevertheless still marked differences in some aspects of UK law compared to national laws in other member states of the Community. Equally, there are still marked differences between UK national law and European law as defined, primarily, by the Treaty of Rome. This chapter will explore how UK law interacts with the Treaty of Rome and how the former is likely to change over the next few years in order to bring it into line with that of other member states.

UK law and the Treaty of Rome

Since the underlying concept of a trading community such as the EEC is the free movement of goods, it is immediately apparent that a dichotomy exists between this principle and the general right of an intellectual property owner to exercise that right against a third party and thus prevent, for example, the sale of a patented product in a member state where the patent rights exist, or the importation of a product under a trade mark from one member state into another where the mark has already been registered by someone else. It was mentioned in Chapter 1 that compromises have to be made and in the EEC these are often at the expense of the intellectual property owner. These compromises are built into the Treaty of Rome in, respectively, Articles 30 to 36, 85 and 86.

Import and export between states

Articles 30 to 34 generally deal with the elimination of 'quantitative restrictions' on the import or export of goods between member states of the Community, with Article 35 merely declaring the intention of the member states to remove any existing restrictions as quickly as possible. Article 36 provides the exceptions to these quantitative restrictions and states that:

> The provisions of Articles 30 to 34 shall not preclude prohibitions or restrictions on imports, exports or goods in transit justified on grounds of public morality, public policy or public security; the protection of health and life of humans, animals or plants; the protection of national treasures possessing artistic, historic or archaeological value; or the protection of industrial and commercial property. Such prohibitions or restrictions shall not, however, constitute a means of arbitrary discrimination or a disguised restriction on trade between member states.

Put into plain language, it means that as regards the owners of intellectual property rights the general prohibition on restrictions of imports and exports does not apply if the effect would be an infringement of such rights. Thus, if a UK manufacturer of a product has patented it in the United Kingdom but not in the rest of Europe then he can still prevent imports of the product into the UK but cannot, of course, prevent the sale or use of the product elsewhere in Europe. The same applies if the manufacturer of a product in, say, Italy applies a trade mark (which is almost always the case) to a product and then tries to export it to the UK where someone else already has the trade mark rights. In those circumstances, the importation into the UK can be prevented and, similarly, the owner of the Italian trade mark can prevent the importation into Italy of the product manufactured in the UK.

Parallel importing

This is, however, not quite the end of the matter since any sufficiently large trading community, particularly one composed of a relatively large number of member states, will always experience price differentials for the same product as between different member states. This simple fact has led to a practice popularly referred to as 'parallel importing' of goods (termed 'grey goods'), meaning importation by a third party of goods which are manufactured by or under the authority of the trade mark owner in one country and are then purchased on the open market by the third party, shipped to another country and sold at a profit. European law does not prohibit this even though national law may attempt to. Similarly, the owner of a UK patent cannot prevent the importation into the United Kingdom of a product which it has by itself or with its consent already lawfully put onto the market elsewhere in the Community.

In each case, once the goods are lawfully put in circulation somewhere in the Common Market the rights of the trade mark owner and patent owner, respectively, are said to be exhausted and Article 36 no longer applies.

If confusion results

It should be noted, however, that the situation is different if the parallel importation, particularly of a product bearing a trade mark, results in confusion or deception of the trade or public as to the character or quality of the goods concerned. If this happens, an action for trade mark infringement or passing off under the common law may still be available to the trade mark owner. Such situations usually arise when, despite the fact that the goods are genuine, there is a difference in the nature of the goods or the packaging used in different member states. An example would be if an oil manufacturer sells oil of a relatively low viscosity in one member state having a relatively cold climate, but sells oil of a different viscosity bearing the same trade mark in another member state which has a warmer climate. In each instance the goods are genuine but the sale of the oil designed for the warmer climate in a country having a colder climate could clearly deceive the purchasing public and could also cause damage to vehicle engines in which the oil is used, unless the parallel importer makes it clear that the imported oil is different to the local one.

Similar considerations may apply if different packaging is used in one country as opposed to another if the sale of the product in a country for which it was not intended causes consumers to wonder whether the product is genuine or not. A further example is if the genuine goods are re-packaged by a third party. If the net effect is that confusion or deception arises then the trade mark owner may still be able to take action to prevent the parallel importation.

Despite these examples where the exceptions provided by Article 36 may not apply, in most instances and as a general rule, fair and honest parallel importation into the United Kingdom of products lawfully marketed elsewhere by or with the consent of the trade mark, patent or registered design owner in other member states of the community is permitted.

Common Market rules on competition

Articles 85 and 86 of the Treaty of Rome essentially provide rules on competition within the Common Market, Article 85 prohibiting agreements between two or more parties which have as their object or effect the prevention, restriction or distortion of competition and particularly those agreements which:

1. directly or indirectly fix purchase or selling prices or any other trading conditions;
2. limit or control production, markets, technical development, or investments;
3. share markets or sources of supply;
4. apply dissimilar conditions to equivalent transactions with other trading parties, thereby placing them at a competitive disadvantage;
5. make the conclusion of contracts subject to acceptance by the other parties of supplementary obligations which, by their nature or, according to commercial usage, have no connection with the primary subject of such contracts.

Contracts between businesses resident or operating within the Community and which fall into the above categories are automatically void and, significantly, the parties involved can be subjected to very heavy financial penalties if a complaint made to the EEC Commission is upheld.

An example of an agreement which would fall within the prohibitions of Article 85 is a patent licence in which the owner of the patent requires the licensee to purchase raw materials not covered by the patent from a particular source, thus clearly placing the licence into category (5) above. If the owner of the patent is foolish enough to do this he not only risks a fine being imposed by the Commission but, more significantly, may no longer be able to assert the patent against anyone, including the existing licensee.

Similarly, Article 86 can give rise to the same effect as Article 85, since it prohibits the 'abuse of a dominant position' held by a business if the abuse affects trade between member states. The abuses may consist of:

1. directly or indirectly imposing unfair purchase or selling prices or other unfair trading conditions;
2. limiting production, markets or technical development to the prejudice of consumers;
3. applying dissimilar conditions to equivalent transactions with other trading parties, thereby placing them at a competitive disadvantage;
4. making the conclusion of contracts subject to acceptance by the other parties of supplementary obligations which, by their nature or according to commercial usage, have no connection with the primary subject of such contracts.

In reality, Articles 85 and 86 say the same thing, unfair trading practices are prohibited within the EEC if trade between member states is adversely affected. Since the penalties for infringing either Article are severe, important contracts between two or more companies operating within the EEC should be notified by the parties to the Commission for them to determine whether or not the contractual terms are considered satisfactory. This also applies to contracts concerning intellectual property such as patent and know-how licences, particularly those which include provisions for the cross-licensing of technology between two or more businesses operating in different locations within the Community.

Guidelines on patent and know-how licensing

In an ideal world, all such contracts would be notified to the Commission but, of course, there are limitations on manpower and in reality this is impractical. Instead, the Commission has issued Regulation 2349/84 giving guidelines on what clauses in patent and know-how licensing agreements it considers acceptable, with the object of reassuring parties to agreements which contain such acceptable clauses that the entire agreement is valid under EEC law. This effectively provides 'negative clearance' for the parties involved, although it should be noted that incorporating legally acceptable clauses into a contract which includes one or more illegal clauses still places the agreement in breach of, specifically, Article 85.

The clauses considered acceptable under the Regulation are those which include one or more of the following obligations as between two, but no more than two, parties:

1. an obligation on the licensor not to license other parties to exploit the licensed invention in the licensed territory, covering all or part of the Common Market, in so far and as long as one of the licensed patents remain in force;
2. an obligation on the licensor not to exploit the licensed invention in the licensed territory himself in so far and as long as one of the licensed patents remain in force;
3. an obligation on the licensee not to exploit the licensed invention in territories within the Common Market which are reserved for the licensor, in so far and as long as the patented product is protected in those territories by equivalent patents;
4. an obligation on the licensee not to manufacture or use the licensed product, or use the patented process or the know-how, in territories within the Common Market which are licensed to other licensees, in so far and as long as the licensed product is protected in those territories by equivalent patents;
5. an obligation on the licensee not to pursue an active policy of putting the licensed product on the market in the territories within the Common Market which are licensed to other licensees, and in

particular not to engage in advertising specifically aimed at those territories or to establish any branch or maintain any distribution depot there, in so far and as long as the licensed product is protected in those territories by equivalent patents;

6. an obligation on the licensee not to put the licensed product on the market in the territories licensed to other licensees within the Common Market for a period not exceeding five years from the date when the product is first put on the market within the Common Market by the licensor or one of his licensees, in so far as and for as long as the product is protected in those territories by equivalent patents; and
7. an obligation on the licensee to use only the licensor's trade mark or the get-up (e.g. style and colour of product packaging) of the licensor to distinguish the licensed product, provided that the licensee is not prevented from identifying himself as the manufacturer of the product.

The above list of exemptions to clauses which may otherwise be considered illegal provides businesses having dealings in patents and know-how with a reasonably adequate framework for entering into contractual commitments with other parties without fear of recrimination from the European Commission. However, the complexities of European competition law and in particular those relating to technology-related agreements cannot be overemphasized and expert advice from an intellectual property solicitor should be sought before entering into any contract of this nature.

In addition to already regulating contractual terms to preserve the underlying principle of the free movement of goods, European law is set to impact further upon the way in which UK businesses obtain and maintain intellectual property rights in the future. We already have two ways in which patent rights can be obtained in the United Kingdom, one being by applying for a national patent, and the other by applying for a European patent designating the UK as one of the states to which it is to extend. In reality, however, the term 'European patent' is rather misleading since, once granted, it reverts to a bundle of national patent rights which have to be enforced using national laws, albeit under generally uniform guidelines to determine, essentially, what constitutes a validly issued patent and which acts infringe.

Trade marks and registered designs

A similar situation exists with regard to trade marks which are enforced on a national, rather than collective, basis except that UK trade mark law is fundamentally of a different character to the national trade mark laws operating in most of mainland Europe. The reason for this is historical, with the United Kingdom relying upon common law principles to confer ownership of trade marks on a 'first to use' basis, and with most of Europe relying upon Code Napoleon practice generally only to recognize rights through a registration system based on 'first to file'.

Again, UK registered designs only extend to the United Kingdom and certain present or former dependent territories, not the rest of Europe. If equivalent protection is required in Europe then at present this must generally be sought on a country-by-country basis.

All of this has got to change and, significantly, most of the changes will be to bring UK intellectual property laws into line with the rest of Europe. For patents, harmonization will finally be achieved with the implementation of the already drafted Community Patent Convention (the CPC). This provides for a single patent theoretically covering the whole of the Community, although exceptions to ratification of the Treaty can be expected at least initially. It seems inevitable that once the CPC is fully operational, either the European Patent Convention will go or, more likely, national patent offices including the one in the United Kingdom will close.

Similarly, harmonization of trade mark laws is already theoretically well advanced with a Community Trade Mark Convention already in place, but not yet ratified by all member states. The intention is to have a single trade mark registration covering the whole of the Community, although in this case it would be most unlikely if national trade mark registrations are to be superseded by a European registration in view of the long-term nature of trade mark rights, which can hardly be taken away once granted.

The complexities of UK copyright law, including the new design right, will almost certainly provide fertile ground for arguments to arise with business enterprises located in other member states of the Community where equivalent protection is not available.

Conclusions

The foregoing does not mean that every time a change has to be made UK law must necessarily give way to the rest of Europe, but the direction in which all European national laws are to develop is already clear and for owners of intellectual property of whatever kind the next decade is likely to bring with it a host of problems associated with the realignment of national law with 'European law' and consequential difficulties for businesses during the transition period.

Whilst by no means exhaustive, it is hoped that this chapter on European aspects has provided the reader with insights into some of the issues sufficient to illustrate that it is no longer possible to consider UK intellectual property law in isolation to the rest of Europe. For most businesses engaged in trade with the rest of Europe this usually means acquiring and maintaining intellectual property rights outside of, as well as within, the United Kingdom. Of particular importance is the need to register trade marks in advance of the proposed harmonizing legislation, which will attempt to ensure as far as possible that two or more parties within the Community do not share the use of the same trade mark for the same goods or services. Whilst not affecting existing trade mark rights, this policy will lead to a situation where it will become progressively harder to find trade marks which are available for use and registration throughout the whole of the Community since the possible choices of mark will shrink proportionately to the increase in potential registrants. Careful planning of intellectual property requirements for future business within the Community is therefore likely to prove a sound investment and provide a means of taking advantage of the changes to come, whilst at the same time minimizing any potentially adverse consequences for the business.

Appendix 1
A published patent specification

(12) UK Patent (19) GB (11) 2 058 389 B

(54) Title of invention
Optical filter

(51) INT CL^3; **G02B 7/00 5/20**

(21) Application No
8014333

(22) Date of filing
30 Apr 1980

(30) Priority data

(31) **54/109180**

(32) **29 Aug 1979**

(33) **Japan (JP)**

(43) Application published
8 Apr 1981

(45) Patent published
3 Aug 1983

(73) Proprietor
Hoya Corporation,
No. 5—7—2 Nakaochai,
Shinjuku-ku,
Tokyo,
Japan

(72) Inventors
Reiji Motomura,
Hirofumi Ohta,
Takashi Matsuura,
Kou Itaya

(52) Domestic classification
G2J 28 FM

(56) Documents cited
GB 1530209
GB 1447601
GB 1425673
GB 626163

(58) Field of search
G2J
G2X

(74) Agent and/or address for service
Marks and Clerk,
Alpha Tower,
ATV Centre,
Birmingham,
B1 1TT

LONDON THE PATENT OFFICE

GB 2 058 389 B

SPECIFICATION
Optical Filter

This invention relates to optical filters, particularly those for mounting on camera lenses. Optical filters are known which have a frame made of metal, such as aluminum or brass. For instance, the filter shown in partial cross-section in Figure 1 of the accompanying drawings has an annular frame 1 provided with an axially projecting reduced diameter portion defining a flange 2 by means of which the filter can be attached to the lens barrel of a camera. A filter plate 3 has its periphery held against the inner periphery of the flange 2, and a retaining ring 4 is screwed into the frame 1 to retain the filter plate 3 against the flange 2. Alternatively, as shown in Figure 2, the frame 1 is provided along its inner periphery with a stepped annular recess 5 including a larger diameter portion formed along the inner periphery of the flange 2. The filter plate 3 is held in the smaller diameter portion of the annular recess 5 between a stub or stubs or a smaller diameter ring section 5*a*, and a retaining ring 6 of elastic material having a circular or other cross-section is disposed in the larger diameter portion of the recess 5 to retain the filter plate 3 in position. Since in both of these prior constructions the frames are made of metal, the filters are heavy in weight and are also expensive to produce because the elements of the frame require machining. In addition, these filters are difficult to assemble automatically, and require a large amount of human labour for their fabrication. This necessarily adds to the cost of their manufacture.

In order to eliminate these disadvantages of filters having metallic frames, it has recently been proposed to make such frames of a synthetic resin material. A filter having a frame made of a synthetic resin material is light in weight, and is also less expensive to produce since the frame can be press-formed. A typical commercially available filter having a frame 1 formed from a synthetic resin material is shown in Figure 3 of the accompanying drawings. The flange 2 of the frame 1 is formed with an annular ridge 7 along its inner periphery. When the filter is assembled, the annular ridge 7 is elastically deformed to enable forcible insertion of the filter plate 3 into the frame. This type of filter is, however, unsatisfactory since the filter plate 3 fails to be tightly held within the frame, and also because the forcible insertion of the filter plate is likely to cause damage to the ridge 7, thereby impairing the appearance of the filter.

As shown in Figure 4, it is also known to use a filter having a radially inwardly projecting annular flange 8 along the inner periphery of its frame 1, the filter plate 3 being held against the flange 8 and secured thereto and to the inner periphery of the frame 1 with an adhesive 9. This type of filter is also unsatisfactory since, where the filter plate is made of glass, the difference in the co-efficient of expansion between the filter plate and the frame (which is made of a synthetic resin material) is likely to cause detachment of the filter plate from the frame. In addition, exposure of any excess adhesive from the area between the filter plate and the frame is often very detrimental to the overall appearance of the filter.

In all of the above-described conventional filters, the frame is made in a single piece.

It is an object of the present invention to obviate or mitigate the above-described disadvantages of conventional optical filters.

According to one aspect of the present invention, there is provided an optical filter comprising a filter plate held in a frame made of a synthetic resin material, the frame being composed of a pair of co-axially disposed annular parts which are respectively internally and externally screw-threaded, a first of said annular parts having internal screw-threading at one axial end thereof and a connection portion at the other axial end, the second of said annular parts having external screw-threading at one axial end thereof and a connection portion at the other axial end, the first and second parts being secured together by means of their connection portions with the filter plate held therebetween.

Such a filter has a construction which permits its automatical fabrication without requiring any cumbersome manual work. Moreover, the filter can be made light in weight and has a frame and a filter plate which are firmly secured to each other. The filter presents an improved appearance without exposing at all the area over which the filter plate is secured to the frame (for example by means of an adhesive), and the frame can be made adaptable to any reasonable variation in the thickness of the filter plate.

In one particular construction of the filter, the connection portion of the first frame part has an annular recess which receives the connection portion of the second frame part, and the first and second frame parts are internally recessed to receive the periphery of the filter plate. Alternatively, the first frame part can have external screw-threading at both ends thereof, and the second frame part can be externally screw-threaded along its entire axial length so that it can be threadedly engaged with the connection portion of the frame frame part.

At least one of the first and second frame parts can be provided with a saw-toothed or otherwise rugged end configuration in the region where the two parts are secured to each other. This rugged configuration is advantageous for providing a fine appearance to the filter and adapting the frame to different thicknesses of the filter plate, as will be described in detail later. The use of ultrasonic waves is advantageous for achieving an improved strength of adhesion between the various elements of the filter, as well as facilitating automatic fabrication thereof.

According to a second aspect of the present invention, there is provided a method of manufacturing an optical filter as defined in the fourth last preceding paragraph, comprising preparing from a thermoplastic synthetic resin material a first annular frame part having internal screw-threading thereon and a second annular frame part having external screw-threading thereon, disposing a filter plate between the first and second frame parts while inserting the second frame part into the first frame part, and applying ultrasonic waves to at least a part of the area of contact between the first and second frame parts to weld said parts together with the filter plate held therebetween.

The present invention will now be further described, by way of example only, with reference to the remaining Figures of the accompanying drawings, in which:—

Figure 5 is a partial longitudinal cross-section through a first embodiment of an optical filter according to the present invention;

Figure 6 is a similar view to Figure 5 of a second embodiment of an optical filter according to the present invention; and

Figure 7 is a similar view to Figure 5 of a third embodiment of an optical filter according to the present invention.

The optical filter shown in Figure 5 comprises a filter plate 13 and a frame holding the filter plate 13 therein. The frame, which is formed from a thermoplastic synthetic resin material such as acrylonitrile butadiene styrene (ABS) copolymer or polycarbonate, comprises an externally threaded rear portion 11 adapted for attachment to the lens barrel of a camera and an internally threaded front portion 12. The filter plate 13 is held between the front and rear frame portions 12 and 11 which are secured to each other over an area 14. Both the front and rear portions of the frame are simple in shape and can be easily prepared by press-forming. The area 14 over which the two portions 11 and 12 are secured to each other is concealed within the frame and is not visible from the outside thereof. This feature assists in the preparation of a filter having a fine appearance. The connection of the two portions 11 and 12 can be accomplished by using an ordinary adhesive. For instance, where the frame is made of ABS methyl ethyl ketone (MEK) is preferably used as an adhesive. More advantageously, however, the frame portions can be secured together by thermal fusion, preferably by the application of ultrasonic waves (using, for example, a frequency of about 10 KHz) at an appropriate intensity to fuse the resin material in the area 14 to join the two portions integrally. The use of ultrasonic waves is advantageous since it provides a strong attachment between the two frame portions 11 and 12 and facilitates automatic fabrication of the filter.

Figure 6 shows a modified form of the filter shown in Figure 5, likewise having a frame made of a thermoplastic synthetic resin material and composed of a rear portion 11 and a front portion 12 which are integrally connected with each other. In this embodiment, however, the rear portion 11 of the frame is provided with a saw-toothed edge configuration at the connecting end thereof where the rear portion 11 is connected to the front portion 12. The saw-toothed configuration comprises a plurality of projections 15 and a plurality of recesses 15′ which are arranged alternately with the projections 15. This rugged edge configuration provides a number of advantages in the manufacture of the filter. If too much ultrasonic wave energy is applied for the fusion of the resin material to join the two frame portions, there is a likelihood that too much resin material may become molten and swell out of the area of attachment between the two frame portions, thereby impairing the overall appearance of the filter. In the filter shown in Figure 6, however, it is possible to prevent exposure of such excess molten resin material to the exterior of the filter, as all such excess material can be neatly confined within the recesses 15′. The rugged configuration is also advantageous in that it is possible to adapt the two frame portions to any reasonable variation in the thickness of the filter plate 13 without the necessity of using frame portions having different dimensions. If the filter plate 13 has a relatively large thickness, the resin material of the projections 15 is melted to a relatively small extent; if the filter plate 13 has a relatively small thickness, the projections 15 are melted to a larger extent, and any excess molten resin material is confined within the recesses 15′, without leaking out to the exterior of the filter. Typically, the filter plate has a thickness of about 1.7 to 2.5 mm.

Another modified form of the filter is shown in Figure 7, and has a frame composed of a rear portion 11 which is externally threaded along its entire length, and a front portion 12 which is internally threaded at both ends thereof. The rear and front portions 11 and 12 are connected in threaded relationship with each other at 16, and are further joined with an adhesive or by thermal fusion as hereinbefore described. This combined mode of connection provides a very strong attachment between the two frame portions. While such a strong attachment may not be necessary for a filter for ordinary use, it is quite useful for a filter intended for use under special conditions.

Claims

1. An optical filter comprising a filter plate held in a frame made of a synthetic resin material, the frame being composed of a pair of co-axially disposed annular parts which are respectively internally and externally screw-threaded, a first of said annular parts having internal screw-threading at one axial end thereof and a connection portion at the other axial end, the second of said annular parts having external screw-threading at one axial end thereof and a connection portion at the other axial end, the first and second parts being secured together by means of their connection portions with the filter plate held therebetween.

2. An optical filter as claimed in claim 1, wherein the connection portion of the first frame

part has an annular recess which receives the connection portion of the second frame part, and the first and second frame parts are internally recessed to receive the periphery of the filter plate.

3. An optical filter as claimed in claim 1, wherein the first frame part has internal screw-threading at both ends thereof, and the second frame part is externally screw-threaded along its entire axial length and is in screw-threaded engagement with the connection portion of the first frame part.

4. An optical filter as claimed in claim 1, 2 or 3, wherein the connection portions of the frame parts are secured together by adhesive.

5. An optical filter as claimed in claim 1, 2 or 3, wherein the connection portions of the frame parts are thermally fused together.

6. An optical filter as claimed in claim 5, wherein the connection portion of at least one of the frame parts is provided with a plurality of projections alternating with a plurality of recess, and the frame parts are fused together by means of said projections.

7. An optical filter as claimed in claim 6, wherein said projections and recesses are provided on the connection portion of the second frame part.

8. A method of manufacturing an optical filter as claimed in claim 1, comprising preparing from a thermoplastic synthetic resin material a first annular frame part having internal screw-threading thereon and a second annular frame part having external screw-threading thereon, disposing a filter plate between the first and second frame parts while inserting the second frame part into the first frame part, and applying ultrasonic waves to at least a part of the area of contact between the first and second frame parts to weld said parts together with the filter plate held therebetween.

9. A method as claimed in claim 8, further comprising the step of forming at least one of the frame parts with a plurality of projections around one end thereof, the ultrasonic waves being applied to these projections.

10. A method as claimed in claim 8, wherein the second frame part is inserted in threaded relationship into the first frame part.

11. An optical filter substantially as hereinbefore described with reference to any one of Figures 5 to 7 of the accompanying drawings.

12. A method of manufacturing an optical filter, substantially as hereinbefore described with reference to any one of Figures 5 to 7 of the accompanying drawings.

Printed for Her Majesty's Stationery Office by the Courier Press, Leamington Spa, 1983. Published by the Patent Office, 25 Southampton Buildings, London, WC2A 1AY, from which copies may be obtained

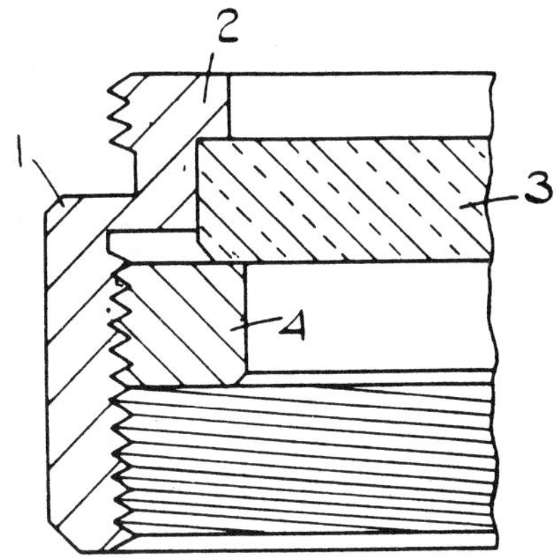

FIG.1.

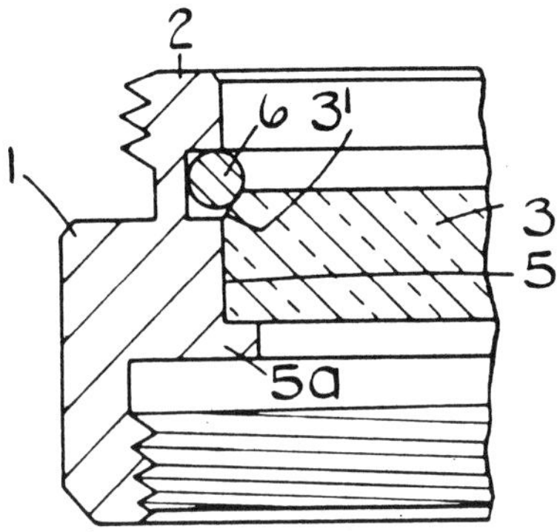

FIG.2.

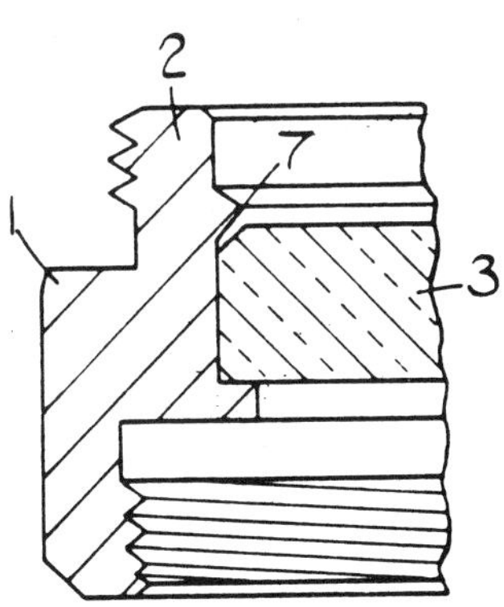

FIG.3.

FIG.4.

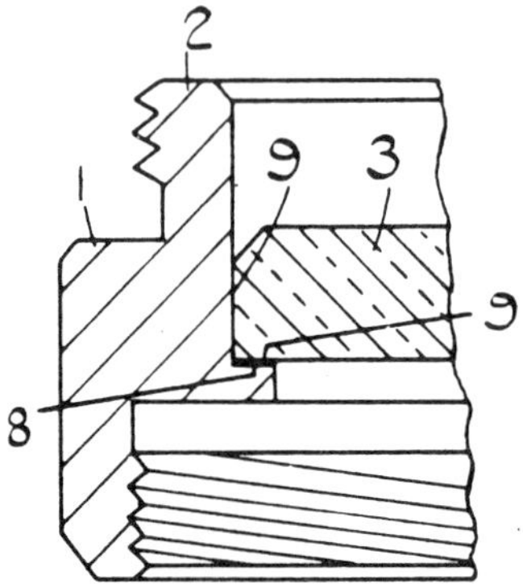

FIG.5.

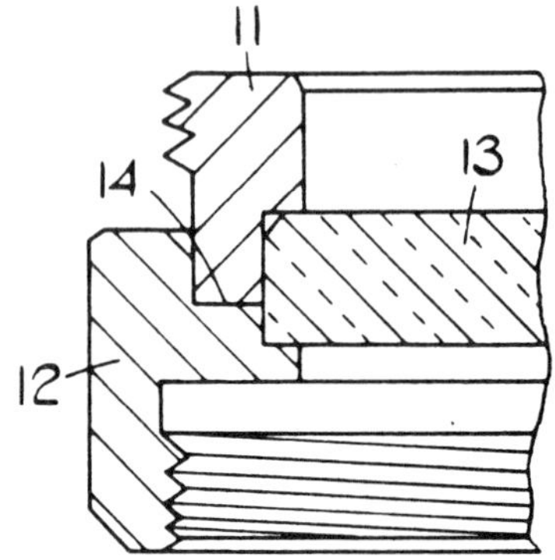

FIG.6.

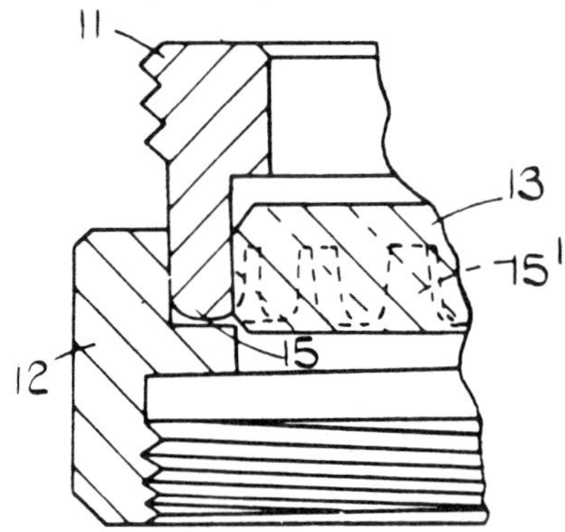

FIG.7.

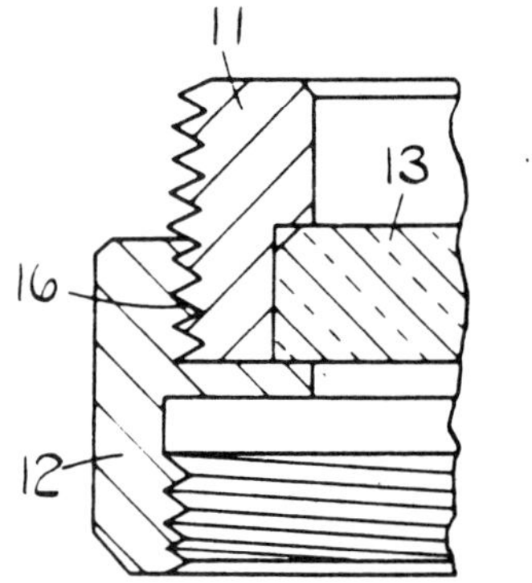

Appendix 2

How accepted trade mark applications are advertised for possible opposition by third parties

INTERNATIONAL CLASSIFICATION OF GOODS AND SERVICES

Class

1. Chemicals used in industry, science and photography, as well as in agriculture, horticulture and forestry; unprocessed artificial resins, unprocessed plastics; manures; fire extinguishing compositions; tempering and soldering preparations; chemical substances for preserving foodstuffs; tanning substances; adhesives used in industry.

2. Paints, varnishes, lacquers, preservatives against rust and against deterioration of wood, colourants; mordants; raw natural resins; metals in foil and powder form for painters, decorators, printers and artists.

3. Bleaching preparations and other substances for laundry use; cleaning, polishing, scouring and abrasive preparations; soaps; perfumery, essential oils, cosmetics, hair lotions; dentifrices.

4. Industrial oils and greases; lubricants; dust absorbing, wetting and binding compositions; fuels (including motor spirit) and illuminants; candles and wicks.

5. Pharmaceutical, veterinary and sanitary preparations; dietetic substances adapted for medical use, food for babies; plasters, materials for dressings; material for stopping teeth, dental wax, disinfectants; preparations for destroying vermin; fungicides, herbicides.

6. Common metals and their alloys; metal building materials; transportable buildings of metal; materials of metal for railway tracks; non-electric cables and wires of common metal; ironmongery, small items of metal hardware; pipes and tubes of metal; safes; goods of common metal not included in other classes; ores.

7. Machines and machine tools; motors and engines (except for land vehicles); machine coupling and transmission components (except for land vehicles); agricultural implements; incubators for eggs.

8. Hand tools and implements (hand operated); cutlery; side arms; razors.

9. Scientific, nautical, surveying, electric photographic, cinematographic, optical, weighing, measuring, signalling, checking (supervision), life-saving and teaching apparatus and instruments; apparatus for recording, transmission or reproduction of sound or images; magnetic data carriers, recording discs; automatic vending machines and mechanisms for coin-operated apparatus; cash-registers, calculating machines, data processing equipment and computers; fire-extinguishers apparatus.

10. Surgical, medical, dental and veterinary apparatus and instruments, artificial limbs, eyes and teeth; orthopaedic articles; suture materials.
11. Apparatus for lighting, heating, steam generating, cooking, refrigerating, drying, ventilating, water supply and sanitary purposes.
12. Vehicles; apparatus for locomotion by land, air or water.
13. Firearms; ammunition and projectiles; explosives; fireworks.
14. Precious metals and their alloys and goods in precious metals or coated therewith, not included in other classes; jewellery, precious stones; horological and chronometric instruments.
15. Musical instruments.
16. Paper, cardboard and goods made from these materials, not included in other classes; printed matter; bookbinding material; photographs; stationery; adhesives for stationery or household purposes; artists' materials; paint brushes; typewriters and office requisites (except furniture); instructional and teaching material (except apparatus); plastic materials for packaging (not included in other classes); playing cards; printers' type; printing blocks.
17. Rubber, gutta-percha, gum, asbestos, mica and goods made from these materials and not included in other classes; plastics in extruded form for use in manufacture; packing, stopping and insulating materials; flexible pipes, not of metal.
18. Leather and imitations of leather, and goods made of these materials and not included in other classes; animal skins, hides; trunks and travelling bags; umbrellas, parasols and walking sticks; whips, harness and saddlery.
19. Building materials (non-metallic); non-metallic rigid pipes for building, asphalt, pitch and bitumen; non-metallic transportable buildings; monuments, not of metal.
20. Furniture, mirrors, picture frames; goods (not included in other classes) of wood, cork, reed, cane, wicker, horn, bone, ivory, whalebone, shell, amber, mother-of-pearl, meerschaum and substitutes for all these materials, or of plastics.
21. Household or kitchen utensils and containers (not of precious metal or coated therewith); combs and sponges; brushes (except paint brushes); brush-making materials; articles for cleaning purposes; steelwool; unworked or semi-worked glass (except glass used in building); glassware, porcelain and earthenware not included in other classes.
22. Ropes, string, nets, tents, awnings, tarpaulins, sails, sacks and bags (not included in other classes); padding and stuffing materials (except of rubber or plastics); raw fibrous textile materials.
23. Yarns and threads, for textile use.
24. Textiles and textile goods, not included in other classes; bed and table covers.
25. Clothing, footwear, headgear.
26. Lace and embroidery, ribbons and braid; buttons, hooks and eyes, pins and needles; artificial flowers.
27. Carpets, rugs, mats and matting, linoleum and other materials for covering existing floors; wall hangings (non-textile).

28. Games and playthings; gymnastic and sporting articles not included in other classes; decorations for Christmas trees.
29. Meat, fish, poultry and game; meat extracts; preserved, dried and cooked fruits and vegetables; jellies, jams, fruit sauces; eggs, milk and milk products; edible oils and fats.
30. Coffee, tea, cocoa, sugar, rice, tapioca, sago, artificial coffee; flour and preparations made from cereals, bread, pastry and confectionery, ices; honey, treacle; yeast, baking-powder; salt, mustard, vinegar, sauces (condiments); spices; ice.
31. Agricultural, horticultural and forestry products and grains not included in other classes; live animals; fresh fruit and vegetables; seeds, natural plants and flowers; foodstuffs for animals, malt.
32. Beers; mineral and aerated waters and other non-alcoholic drinks; fruit drinks and fruit juices; syrups and other preparations for making beverages.
33. Alcoholic beverages (except beers).
34. Tobacco; smokers' articles; matches.
35. Advertising; business management; business administration; office functions.
36. Insurance; financial affairs; monetary affairs; real estate affairs.
37. Building construction; repair; installation services.
38. Telecommunications.
39. Transport; packaging and storage of goods; travel arrangement.
40. Treatment of materials.
41. Education; providing of training; entertainment; sporting and cultural activities.
42. Providing of food and drink; temporary accommodation; medical, hygenic and beauty care; veterinary and agricultural services; legal services; scientific and insutrial research; computer programming; services that cannot be placed in other classes.

(Source: UK *Trade Marks Journal*)

Appendix 3
Extract from the *Trade Marks Journal*

CLASS 28 *continued*

1477659 24 September 1991 (28)

PRINCESS HOUSE

Princess House

Application under Section 21(2) for a series of two marks.

Registration of these marks shall give no right to the exclusive use of the word "House".

To be associated with No. 1465488 (5921,3478).

Toys, games and playthings; dolls and dolls' clothing; accessories for dolls; dolls' furniture; dolls' furniture accessories; parts and fittings for all the aforesaid goods; all included in Class 28.

Princess House, Inc., 455 Somerset Avenue, North Dighton, Massachusetts 02754, United States of America.

Agent: Marks & Clerk, 57–60 Lincoln's Inn Fields, London, WC2A 3LS.

1481145 31 October 1991 (28)

QUINTS COUSINS

Proceeding under Section 29 (1)(b).

To be associated with No. 1413765 (5962,913) and another.

Toys, playthings, dolls and accessories for dolls; all included in Class 28.

Tyco Industries, Inc., 6000 Midlantic Drive, Mount Laurel, New Jersey, 08054, United States of America.

Agent: David Keltie Associates, Audrey House, Ely Place, London, EC1N 6SN.

1425926 20 April 1990 (28)

FLOO MAN CHOO

Registration of this mark shall give no right to the exclusive use of the word "Man".

To be associated with No. 1425925 (5951,8582).

Toys, games and playthings; gymnastic and sporting articles; parts and fittings for all the aforesaid goods; all included in Class 28.

Buggsun Ltd, 3 Mealth Road, Ilford, Essex 1.

Agent: Grant, Spencer, Caisley & Porteous, Metropolis House, 22 Percy Street, London, W1P 9FF.

CLASS 28 *continued*

1424109 2 May 1990 (28)

Registration of this mark shall give no right to the exclusive use of a letter "C".

Toys, games and playthings; dolls' accessories; jigsaw puzzles; card games; board games; adhesive articles and image transfers, all being interchangeable and reuseable and all being sold in kit form; floatable self-adhering forms constructed of foam materials; parts and fittings for all the aforesaid goods; all included in Class 28.

Colorforms, 133 Williams Drive, Ramsey, New Jersey, United States of America.

Agent: Reddie & Grose, 16 Theobalds Road, London, WC1X 8PL.

CLASS 29

1353611 2 August 1988 (29)

Advertised before acceptance. Section 18(1) (proviso).

Fruits and vegetables, all being preserved, dried or cooked; meat for food for human consumption; meat extracts; burgers, faggots, sausages, sausagemeat, black pudding; potato chips, potato crisps; savoury foodstuffs; preparations containing meat, potato or meat and potato; snackfoods, desserts and fillings for the aforesaid snackfoods and desserts; prepared meals and constituents for the aforesaid prepared meals; eggs, scotch eggs; all included in Class 29.

Roy's Cooked Meats Limited, Viking Way, Winch Wen Industrial Estate, Swansea, West Glamorgan, SA1 7DE.

Agent: Frank B. Dehn & Co., Imperial House, 15–19 Kingsway, London, WC2B 6UZ.

(Source: UK *Trade Marks Journal*)

Appendix 4
A trade mark registration certificate

TRADE MARKS ACT, 1938

GREAT BRITAIN AND
NORTHERN IRELAND

NEXT

next

next

The Trade Mark above has been registered in Part A of the Register under No 1256099 as of the date 9 December 1985 in Class 25 Schedule 4 in the name of:

NEXT RETAIL LIMITED

In respect of:
Articles of outerclothing for women; T-shirts, vests and pyjamas, all for women.

The Patent Office, The Trade Marks Registry,
State House
66-71 High Holborn
London WC1R 4TP

Sealed at my direction this
24 day of November 1989

cf. P R S HARTNACK
REGISTRAR

Appendix 5

A Registered Design Certificate

CERTIFICATE OF REGISTRATION OF DESIGN

Number of Registration 2018284

Date of Registration 14th October 1991

Date of grant of Certificate 18th November 1992

This is to certify that,

in pursuance of and subject to the provisions of the Registered Designs Act 1949, the Design, of which a representation or specimen is attached, has been registered as of the date of registration shown above in the name of

United System Limited

in respect of the application of such design to:

Trolley for luggage

Registrar of Designs

Please read the important notes overleaf

DR1/CRD/ACD

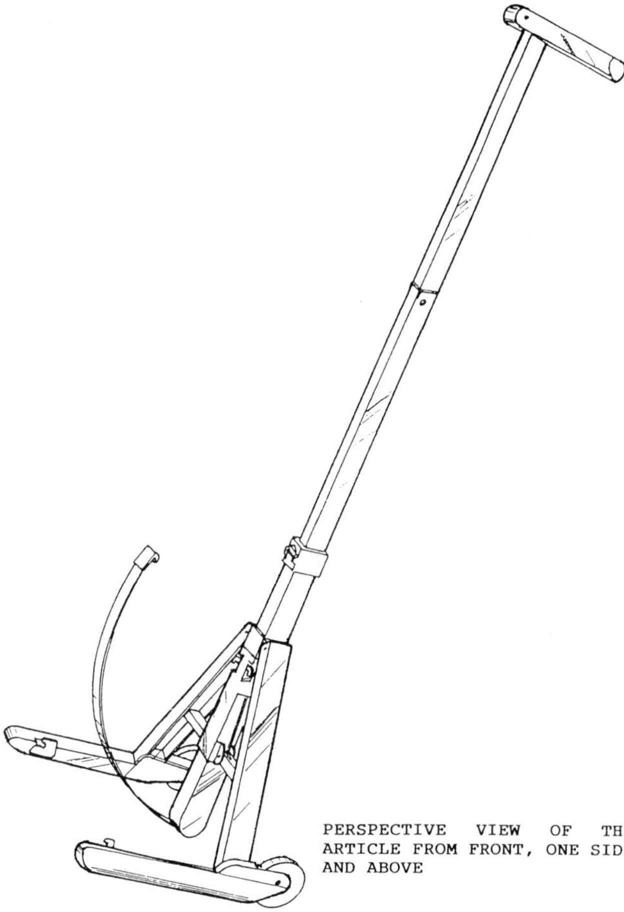

PERSPECTIVE VIEW OF THE ARTICLE FROM FRONT, ONE SIDE AND ABOVE

STATEMENT OF NOVELTY

The features of the design for which novelty is claimed reside in the shape or configuration applied to the article as shown in the representations.

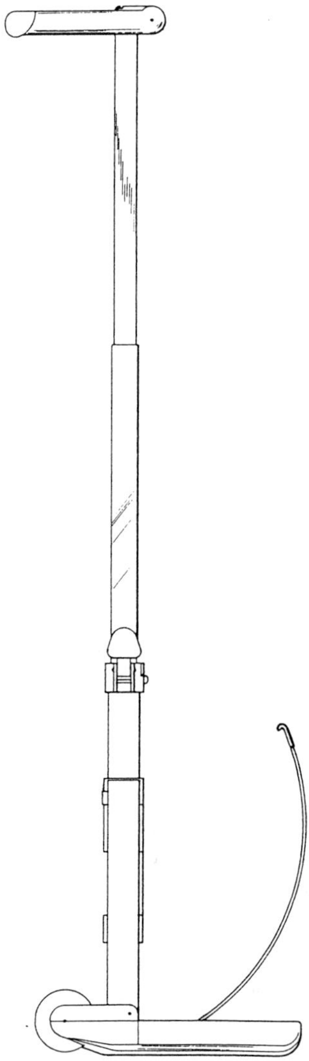

VIEW OF OTHER SIDE

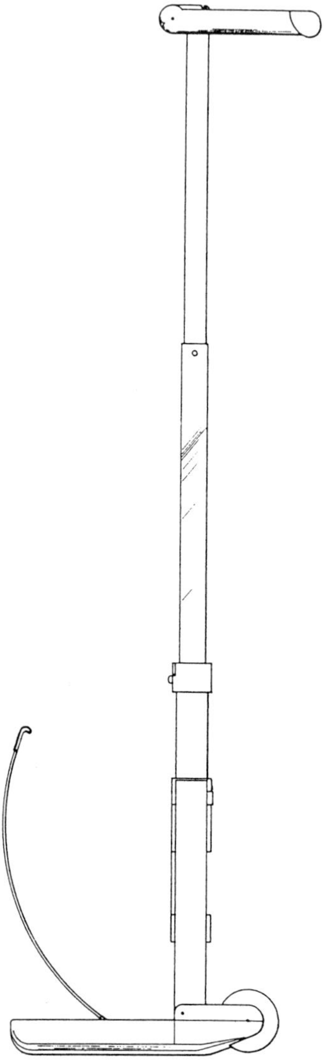

VIEW OF ONE SIDE

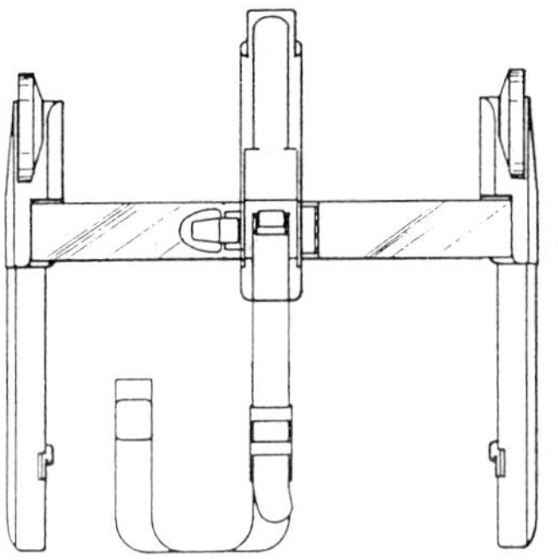

VIEW FROM ABOVE,
WITH STRAP IN
DIFFERENT POSITION

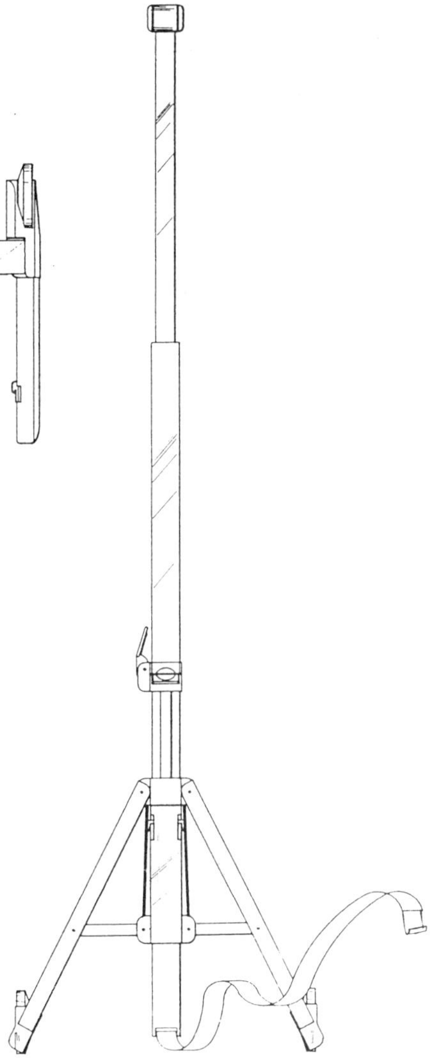

FRONT VIEW, WITH STRAP
IN DIFFERENT POSITION

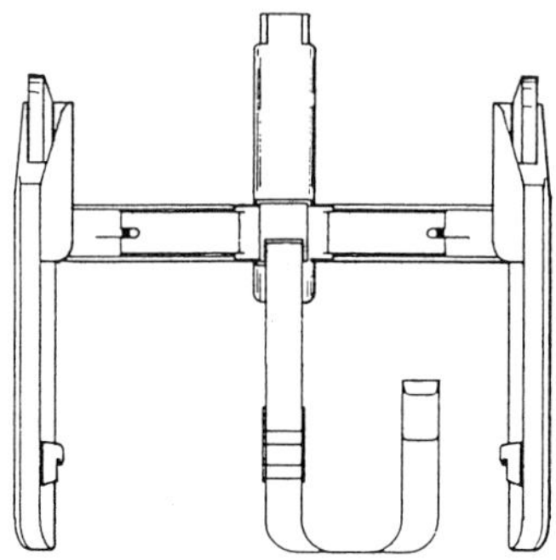

VIEW FROM BELOW, WITH
STRAP IN DIFFERENT POSITION

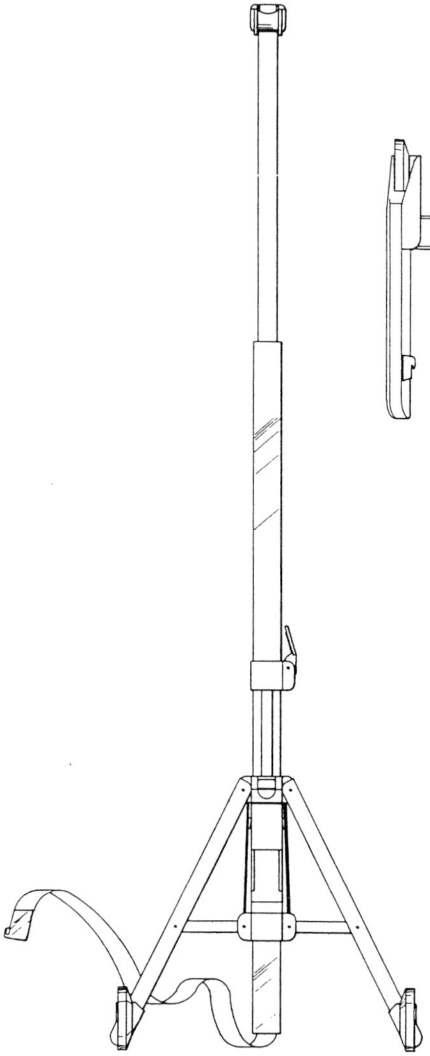

REAR VIEW, WITH STRAP
IN DIFFERENT POSITION

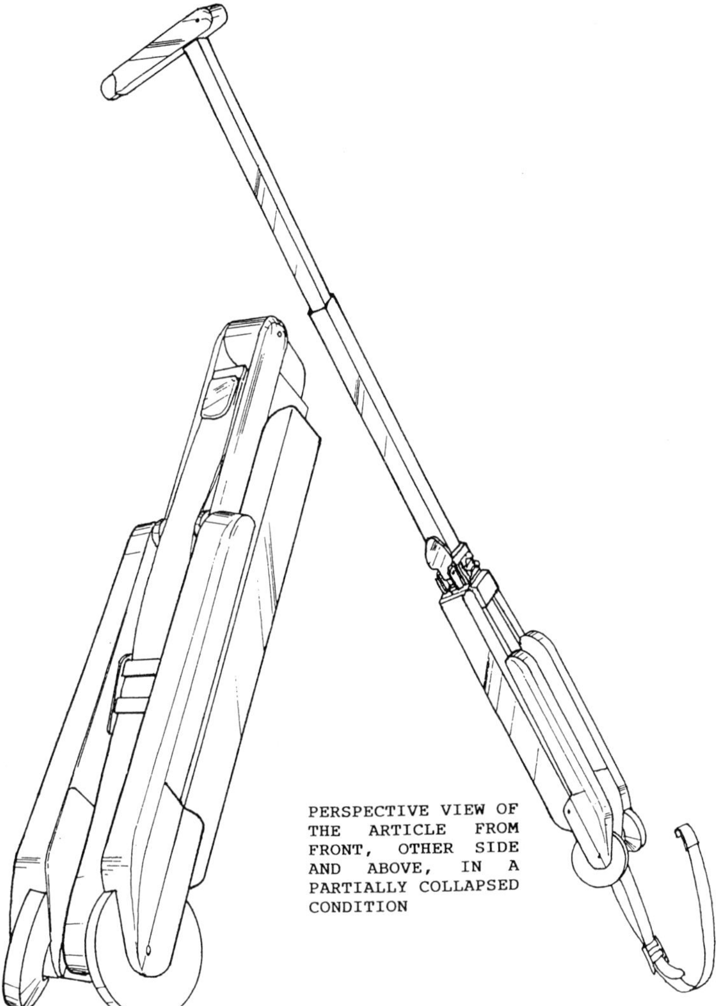

PERSPECTIVE VIEW OF THE ARTICLE FROM FRONT, OTHER SIDE AND ABOVE, IN A PARTIALLY COLLAPSED CONDITION

ENLARGED PERSPECTIVE VIEW OF THE ARTICLE FROM FRONT, ONE SIDE AND ABOVE, IN A FULLY COLLAPSED CONDITION

Index